Crystal Saga
Tamara's Crystals and Genesis Explored

D. E. Weingand

Crystal Saga
Tamara's Crystals and Genesis Explored
A Crystal Saga Series

Copyright © 2021 by D. E. Weingand
All rights reserved

ISBN: 978-0-578-99539-7
Tamara's Crystals Library of Congress: TX 9-043-538

Published by D. E. Weingand, Florence, Oregon 97439.

Printed in the United States of America.

Publisher's Note: This book is a work of fiction. Names, characters, places, and incidents are either the product of the author's imagination or are used fictitiously, and any resemblance to actual persons, living or dead, events, or locales is entirely coincidental.

Front cover photo by D. E. Weingand.

Luanna K. Leisure, Little White Feather Graphic Artist and Independent Publisher.

To order additional books go to: **http://www.LuLu.com, Amazon.com or Barnesandnoble.com**

Email: weingand@me.com

Tamara's Crystals
A Crystal Saga Series
Book 1

Table of Contents

Cast of Characters v

Setting and Geography vii

Dedication and Acknowledgements viii

Prologue xi

1. Seven Years Later 1
2. Beneath the Sea 5
3. Meeting Solange 13
4. Lessons 21
5. The Great Awakening 29
6. A New Order 43
7. Tamara's Powers 53
8. The Power of Crystals 59
9. Plotting and Planning 65
10. The Reception 71
11. Decoding a Puzzle 83
12. The Puzzle Deepens 99
13. Sharing Ideas and Strategies 107
14. Preparing Defenses 115

Genesis Explored
A Crystal Saga Series
Book 2

Table of Contents

Prologue iii
1. Dreamscape 1
2. Interpretation Begins 7
3. Continuation 13
4. Joining Forces 19
5. Of Magic and Magicians 27
6. The Breakfast Meeting 37
7. Return of Sunan 43
8. From Conjecture to Evidence 51
9. An Unanticipated Twist 59
10. Attention to the Three-Pronged Plan 65
11. More Evidence to Consider 71
12. The Ball 77
13. More Plotting and Planning 89
About the Author 101
Coming Soon 103

Cast of Characters

Tamara…Heroine of Book 1 and beyond

Terra…Tamara's mother

Trident…Tamara's father and first a prince and then King of Marinea

Trina…Tamara's sister

Mia…Tamara's personal attendant

            *   *   *   *   *

Solange…Tamara's grandmother and a Super Daughter/Sister, advisor to the throne of Marinea. Has fair skin, and silver hair and eyes like Marineans. Wields white magic. Twin to Savea.

Savea… Super Daughter/Sister and Solange's twin, lives near a volcano. Has dark skin, hair and eyes unlike Marineans.

Sostor…a Super Son/Brother and ice mage and ruler of Mosshire. Has fair skin, blonde hair and very blue eyes like residents of Mosshire. Twin to Sunan.

Sunan…a Super Son/Brother and Sostor's twin. A solar magic mage and ruler of Mesarra. Has dark skin, hair and eyes like residents of Mesarra.

* * * * *

Dr. Astarte…a medical doctor serving the royal court

Dr. Angelus…a medical doctor and Doctor of Magical Studies, serving the royal court.

Brise. . .a member of Security

Setting and Geography

Akura…the planet

Alteria…the land kingdom which succumbed to the Great Quakes and now is an island governed by a Council of Elders. Alterians have hazel eyes and blonde hair. No contact has been made between Alteria and Marinea for generations.

Marinea…a kingdom under the sea formed after the Great Quakes sank the major portion of the land kingdom of Alteria. Marineans have silver hair and eyes and are governed by a king. They have retractable gills created by the Super Sisters in order to live on both land and sea.

Mosshire…a land kingdom in the cold north composed of small pieces of forested and ice-covered land joined by bridges, ruled by Sostor, an ice mage. Residents have fair skin, blonde hair and very blue eyes.

Mesarra…a land kingdom in the south composed of a great desert. Residents are from tribes ruled by Sunan, a solar mage. Residents have very dark hair, skin and eyes.

Dedication

To my friend and Friend of the Honolulu Branch of the National League of American Pen Women, Baerbel Miller. She continued to prod me to complete this book and I hope she can read it in heaven, where she now resides.

Acknowledgements

I would like to thank members of the National League of American Pen Women, from both the Santa Clara and Honolulu branches, who have encouraged me in the writing of these books.

I would also like to thank my daughter, Judith Weston, for her careful reading of the first draft. By catching errors, pointing out inconsistencies, making stylistic suggestions and asking astute questions, she enhanced both the text and the plot.

Crystal Saga
Tamara's Crystals

D. E. Weingand

Prologue

I'm Tamara ... and I used to have a normal life. Until I was around 10 seasons old, I lived in a cottage near the sea on the island of Alteria with my mother and younger sister, Trina. I went to school most days and liked it a lot. Even the exercise classes, although I always avoided taking showers with the other girls. That might seem silly, but I didn't want anyone to notice that I was different. More about that later.

My parents met on the beach. My mother was walking on the sand one day when she noticed someone walking toward her. It was my father and there was an immediate attraction between them. They continued to walk the beach together day after day until they decided to join their lives together and marry. I never knew what my father did for a living, but it seemed like a mystery. No one ever talked about it.

My story really begins with the preparations for my tenth birthday party and, like every year, I was desperately hoping that my father would return from the sea. He left one night [my mother tells me] when I was very young and my sister was just a baby ... and we never saw him again. My mother gazes out to sea and watches the horizon every day and the longing on her face just breaks my heart. I put my arms around her and we look out to the sea together, but all we can see are passing sea birds and the occasional dolphins and whales. Local fisher folk have never found any sign of my father and the mystery continues.

Ever since I was a babe, my hair has been white. Since I spend a lot of time walking on the shore, my skin has tanned to a nice golden shade, which makes my hair look even paler. It has become smooth and straight and half-way down my back. None of my friends have hair like mine ... instead, they have wonderful colors like brown, black, red and yellow. [Even my sister has yellow hair—and it's curly, too!] This does make me feel like an outsider sometimes. Which is why I only take private showers. While other girls have a dent on their stomach [they call it a 'belly button'], I have a crystal in that spot. No one has ever seen it, not even my sister, Trina. I'm very careful. My mother knows, of course, since I've had it all my life. Now that I am almost ten, she says we "have to have a talk." Since we talk all the time, I don't know what she means.

After the birthday party guests departed and we had cleaned up the cottage, mother came into my bedroom and sat on the bed. "Tamara," she said, "You are almost coming of age. There are things that you must know about your father and about yourself. Let's start with your father.

"I've told you that he went to sea one night and never

returned. While it is true that he has not come back, he was not a fisherman. He also was not from Alteria.

"Everyone that you know on our island of Alteria we call Alterians. But this is not the only race of beings on our world. Alterians are the land dwellers that inhabit this island. Far across the sea and also beneath the sea are other lands whose peoples are similar but not exactly like us. Have you studied the cosmology of our world in school?"

"Yes, Mother." I replied.

"Please tell me what you have learned," Mother asked.

"Well, in the beginning there was a Creator Being that made this world that we call Akura, as well as all of the stars and other planets in our universe. But the Creator Being did not like being alone in the midst of all that had been created and longed to share the splendor with someone. So, one day, the Creator Being decided to split some of the Creative essence into two complementary parts, male and female. Thus, in addition to the Creator Being, there were now two Super Beings, separate individuals yet joined by a silver cord so that they could also channel their power into one. The male's personal power was centered in a black crystal and he had dominion over the night, the moons and the stars; the female's crystal was white and she controlled the day with its twin golden suns.

"They lived in a crystal castle atop the tallest mountain on Akura that could only be reached by climbing a crystal staircase. There was a room in the center of the castle that housed a large crystal orb of power. It was in this room where they controlled all of creation. This crystal captured light from the twin suns and showered the earth with rainbows. It was an idyllic time.

"Legends tell us that in the dim past," I continued, "the Super Beings decided to make offspring. Focusing the light of their two crystals onto the crystal orb of power, they each created an additional Super Being in the image of themselves: one male and one female. To each child they gave a personal crystal orb of power. But then they worried that these children might control too much power and not use it wisely, so they split the essence of each child into two parts, creating mirror images of each child. They also split the original crystal orbs given to the Super Beings into two, thereby reducing the power of each child by half. Now there were two male offspring and two female, each set comprising an original and a mirror Super Child, all with significant but not extraordinary powers.

"As this transformation transpired and the power orbs given to the original two children cracked in two, small crystal shards were left alongside. The parents fashioned the pieces of each broken orb into crystal pendants encased in precious metals: gold for the original children and silver for the mirror images."

"Do you know what happened to those crystal shards?" asked Mother.

"No," I replied. "It is said that a great whirlwind arose, captured the shards, and rose into the sky until it could no longer be seen. The fate of those shards continues to remain a mystery."

"Now, what do you know of our planet?" questioned Mother.

I continued, "Originally all the lands on Akura were joined into one large continent and the Parent Super Beings gave their children authority over both land and sea. In return, they expected homage and obedience. However, even though the children were endowed with power crystal pendants, they were also subject to the insecurities and rivalries of siblings. They began to argue and fight over who was the strongest, the best looking, and so forth. They fractured the harmony of the family and the Parent Super Beings were very displeased.

"Punishment was necessary, so the Parent Super Beings took a nearby asteroid and hurled it at Akura. The four children were terrified, but used their crystal pendants to focus power at the asteroid, attempting to deflect it before it could destroy them. They were only partially successful. The asteroid broke into pieces: each piece became a moon that now orbits our planet and gives light to our night.

"Relieved that the danger seemed to be past, the Super Children shed many tears which fell on the ground, each tear becoming a being with no powers. These various peoples multiplied and learned to live in harmony. In their innocence, they began to view the Super Children as deities worthy of worship. But the Parent Super Beings were jealous of that misdirected piety and caused a series of Great Quakes that split the unified land mass into three major pieces. One of the pieces had another severe tremor and sunk beneath the sea, leaving only a small island in its wake—our Alteria.

"The Parent Super Beings then separated their children, giving the two Super Sons control over the land, each residing on one of the remaining large land masses. The two Super Daughters were given the sea as their home and developed gills. The children were told that, while their parents would always be watching over them, the sons and daughters would be left alone to look after Akura for many millennia as part of their education. The crystal palace would be hidden from their eyes until that future date when they would all be reunited."

"You have learned well, my daughter," said Mother. "But remember that these land masses drifted far apart over time and the peoples have evolved quite differently. In the north there are many small pieces of land connected by bridges. Some are forested but most are covered with ice. This kingdom is called Mosshire and is ruled by one of the Super Sons, a sorceror named Sostor, who is a master of ice magic. Mosshireans have fair skin, blonde hair and very blue eyes, like Sostor.

"To the south live the Mesarreans on a great desert that stretches for many leagues in all directions. These folk belong to many tribes that are loosely joined into a confederation called Mesarra and ruled by the other Super Son, Sunan, serving as Mage here and as a master of solar magic. Like Sunan, the Mesarreans tend to have eyes, skin and hair that are quite dark.

"Finally, under the sea are beings known as Marineans who are quite different from all land folk. They are the descendants of those who had lived on the land that was pulled beneath the sea. At the time of the Great Quake, they were governed by a king. Since their kingdom sank beneath the sea, they have been advised by the two Super Daughters who were able to cast a spell that enabled the people to survive at the bottom of the ocean. Marineans have silver hair and eyes. The people who remained on our island of Alteria have changed in appearance and tend to have hazel eyes and blonde hair. They have always been governed by a Council of Elders and have not had contact with their undersea cousins for many generations. Your father is a Marinean prince and would spend time both under the sea and with us here on land."

I gasped. "You mean that's why I'm different from my friends?" I asked. "I look like my father?"

"Yes," Mother said, "Although your hair is white, not silver, and your eyes seem to capture many colored highlights."

"How can my father live under the sea? Won't he drown? And why did he go there and never come home?"

"Marineans can live comfortably under the sea because, like fish, they were given gills by the Super Daughters with which to breathe when submerged in water," replied her mother. "On land, the gills retract and are not visible."

"So the Marineans have gills and can breathe underwater. But we Alterians are from the same race of people, so can we live in the sea, too?" asked Tamara.

"I don't think so, since there was no need for the Super Daughters to change us as we remained on land. But I'm not certain of that. As to why your father left, he received a message that his father –your grandfather--was very ill and he immediately returned to the sea. I don't know what has happened because he has never returned."

"I didn't know I had a grandfather! Why have I never met him?"

"I know that he has been busy ruling the kingdom and we,

of course, live on land. That's not an excuse, just a reason. Your father has tried very hard to create a balance between these two different worlds and it has been hard on him.

"One more thing: Your father told me that the two Super Daughters living beneath the sea had an argument many years ago and no longer work together. Solange is a sorceress and commands white or good magic. She remains in the palace of the king and, you have probably realized, the Marineans resemble Solange in appearance. She is also your father's mother and therefore your grandmother.

"The other twin, Savea, has dark eyes and hair and considers herself unique since she does not resemble any of the undersea dwellers. She dwells near an undersea volcano. The tremors that we often feel are probably her doing."

"So," I responded, "One undersea Super Daughter is good and the other is vengeful. And on land, are the two Super Sons good or bad?"

"I would say," Mother replied, "that they are capable of either behavior depending on what they want. They are moody and temperamental beings, super or not. The only consistently good one of the four Super Children is Solange, the sorceress of white magic that lives in the undersea palace.

"But enough of our cosmology. What is necessary for you to know now concerns the changes that you are about to experience as you come of age. Since you clearly resemble your father, you may develop gills within the next few years.if you don't have some already."

"How can I tell?" I asked.

"You wouldn't be able to tell unless you submerged yourself in the sea," she replied.

My head was spinning with all this information and I had to sit down next to mother on the bed. When I collected myself, I pressed on, "What about my crystal? Where did I get it? What does it do?"

"I'm not sure," she said. "Your father didn't have one, but when you were born, he told me that you were very special and your crystal meant that you would do great things for the Marinean people. He was so proud of you. When he left that night, he made me promise to keep knowledge of your crystal secret from everyone, including your sister. It hasn't been easy, but I've honored his request."

"So now what do I do, Mother? Do I just wait for something to happen to the crystal? Do I swim in the sea to check for gills? Is there some other change that I should be looking for? Please advise me," I pleaded.

Mother sighed and held me close. "I wish I knew, little one. We're in uncharted territory now. If only your father were here."

Chapter 1
Seven Years Later

Tamara stretched languidly and glanced toward the window of her bedroom. Today was her seventeenth birthday and her mother had planned another party, as she had done every year of Tamara's life. The sun was rising with an incandescent glow as dawn crept toward daylight. The sound of birds twittering broke the stillness of the night and the first rays of morning spilled across the floor.

Today, as she had done each birthday since that fateful talk with her mother, she would enter the sea and dive into the deep. Each prior year, she had swum away from the beach and as far underwater as her lungs would allow … and each time she had surfaced gasping for air. Perhaps this year would be different.

Slowly she swung her legs to the floor, stood, and stretched again. *This was surely going to be a good day*! Raising her nightgown over her head, she tossed it on the bed and caught a glimpse of herself in the dresser mirror. With a shriek, she looked down at the crystal on her stomach. It was glowing! This had never happened before. Throwing on a bathrobe, she ran from the room and knocked on her mother's bedroom door.

"Mother, please wake up!" she cried.

"What's the matter?" her mother asked. "You are so pale…and your beautiful hair seems to be glowing!"

"So is my crystal!" Tamara wailed. "What is happening to me?"

"I don't know, darling. How are you feeling?"

"Scared! Look, my crystal is turning yellow!"

"And so is your hair. Say, didn't you always want to be a blonde?"

"Yes, but the kids at school are REALLY going to think I'm weird now. But I do look more like my sister now. I know, I'll tell people that I dyed my hair!"

"That will only work if your hair continues to stay one color. I think you had better stay home from school today and we'll keep an eye on you. Since it's your birthday, why don't you go down to the shore for a while … it's a beautiful day for a walk."

* * * * *

After changing into a swimsuit, Tamara ran out the front door and down the trail to the beach. Her mother had been right: the sky was so blue with high puffy clouds and the sea was a gorgeous shade of turquoise. Two sandpipers were walking on the sand, leaving their curious little footprints to be washed away by the surf. She spun around and splashed happily in the water. A few strands of hair blew across her face—green hair! Stunned, she flopped on the sand and pulled a handful of hair to where she could see it. It was green—all of it! *This certainly was going to be a birthday to remember*, she thought.

Rolling down the waistband of her swimsuit, she peeked at her crystal. It was green, too! There definitely seemed to be a connection between the crystal and her hair color. Interesting, very interesting. She lay back on the sand and watched the clouds move slowly overhead while she pondered this new development. The sound of the ocean waves breaking gently on the shore was very soothing and soon, she was asleep.

Dreams of floating and flying caused her to toss and turn as she lay on the sand. Jolted suddenly awake, she felt the ground shiver and shake and start to undulate. Terrified, she leapt to her feet and started running toward home screaming, "Mother! Trina! Are you all right?"

She stumbled as the tremors increased and a huge crack in the earth appeared just ahead. The world was turning upside down and the noise was deafening. She couldn't move further inland, so she ran along the beach parallel to the water. Glancing up the hill toward the cottage, she fell to her knees in terror. The cottage was gone!

Tamara couldn't believe her eyes. Her cottage home had

completely vanished! *What had happened to her mother and sister? Were they in the cottage or had they managed to escape?* She still couldn't move inland toward where the cottage had been, so she ran farther on down the beach until the crack caused by the quake narrowed to the point where she could jump across it. Scrambling up the hill, she finally reached the site of the cottage to find a huge sinkhole—and no cottage! The hole seemed to have no bottom! She cried out again, "Mother, Trina…where are you?"

There was only silence, deep and frightening. She didn't know what to do. Her crystal was pulsating now with deep yellow hues. Falling to her knees and holding her head in her hands, she began to sob violently. Exhausted, she finally raised her head and looked around. The sky was no longer blue but had changed to a gunmetal gray. There was no sign of life: no birds, no dolphins, no people. The world seemed to be standing still. There was a faint rumble in the distance and she looked around to see where it might be coming from. Over the ocean the clouds were beginning to build and the wind began to howl. Far out to sea, the water started to churn and boil. A wave began to grow in height and speed, moving faster and faster toward the shore. Tamara watched in awe and horror. There was nowhere to run …

Chapter 2
Beneath the Sea

Tamara slowly opened her eyes and looked around. She was lying on some soft cushions and the light surrounding her was a soothing blue-green. *Where am I?* she wondered. The walls were covered with curtains of a soft green fabric. From behind one of the curtains came the sound of a woman's voice, "May I enter?" she asked.

"Yes, of course," replied Tamara.

A young woman about Tamara's age and carrying a bowl of fruit came into the room. "Welcome to Marinea," she said. "My name is Mia. Would you like some refreshment?"

"Thank you. Do you also have something to drink?"

"Of course. There is a pitcher of wine on the sideboard. Is there anything else that you require?"

"Some answers would be great," commented Tamara. "Where am I? What am I doing here?"

"All will be made clear in time," Mia said. "I have been assigned to see to your needs. You will find new clothing in that cabinet against the wall. You can tend to personal hygiene behind the far screen. Dinner will be served in thirty minutes.

I'll return to escort you to the dining room." She turned and slipped behind the curtain.

Tamara walked over to the cabinet and opened the door. "*My goodness*," she thought. Certainly the clothing she found did not look anything like what she was accustomed to wearing. She selected some pantaloons and a flowing caftan, both in a marvelous shade of aquamarine. "*These clothes certainly feel comfortable*," she mused as she put them on. Looking behind the screen, she found a sink and washed her face and hands. There was a brush on a counter and she tackled her hair with long strokes. Her hair was still yellow, but it also had some streaks of blue. Curious.

She peeked behind the door that Mia had used to enter the room and saw a long corridor paved with colorful tiles. "*This certainly is an interesting place, whatever and wherever it is*," she muttered to herself.

It was exactly thirty minutes when Mia reappeared and commented, "You look very lovely, my lady." They walked together down the corridor until they came to a silver door covered with images of dolphins and sea stars. "How beautiful!" Tamara exclaimed. Slowly the doors swung open to reveal a long dinner table and a back wall featuring multiple aquariums. Walking toward them with arms outstretched was a tall, very handsome man with silver hair and eyes. Looking at him was like seeing herself in a mirror—except for the silver coloration, of course.

"Tamara, you are so beautiful," he cried. "Father?" Tamara asked.

"Yes, daughter," said her father. "I'm so glad that you are safe. That was a very powerful tsunami."

"But what happened? The last thing I remember is that really big wave," wondered Tamara.

"It certainly was, and it was caused by another earthquake far offshore from you. You were swept out to sea and some of our people found you and brought you here," added her father. "So I didn't drown?" she asked. "No, obviously," he said with a twinkle in his eye. "But a land dweller would have."

"I'm a land dweller," she replied.

"But you are also my daughter. Your gills saved you."

"My gills? I really have gills? I've been trying to see if I had any for years, but I would always come to the ocean's surface sputtering and gasping."

"No doubt, but now you have come of age and your gills are clear proof of your genetic heritage," said Father.

Tamara put her hands on her face and neck. "I don't feel any gills, but –that's right! Mother said they retract when one is not under water."

"Yes, that's true," said Father. "Shall we go in to dinner?"

"But I have so many questions," Tamara complained as they walked to the dinner table.

"There's plenty of time to talk over dinner and into the evening," remarked Father, pulling out a chair for his daughter. "Our menu tonight is sea bass with shrimp. I'm sure you will enjoy it. And for dessert: seaweed custard."

Tamara mentally shivered at the thought of Father's dessert choice, but her adventurous spirit made her ready for anything! She looked around the room. The table was huge, easily seating twenty or more, yet she and her father were the only diners.

"Father, do you know what happened to mother and my sister? Our cottage was swallowed up by a sinkhole."

"Yes, Tamara. The sinkhole went all the way down to the sea. We were able to find them and secure them from further injury, but I'm afraid they are both still unconscious. Your mother, as you know, is a land dweller and thus has no way to survive naturally under the sea. And it's too early to know whether your sister will have gills or not, so she must be considered a land dweller as well. You can see them after dinner if you wish. We are hoping that this lack of consciousness is temporary. We have excellent medical care here in the palace."

"Palace? That's where we are? Will you show me around

after we eat?"

"Of course. Now let's enjoy our meal."

*   *   *   *   *

Sometime later, Tamara and her father began their tour of the palace, which was constructed of a multicolored coral reef and algae. Coating the inside of the reef was a material that glowed with luminescence and kept the ocean at bay. Tamara asked about the glowing material.

"It's the surface of a bubble of air that was created by the two Sisters when they were still on speaking terms."

"Sisters? Are they the same as Super Daughters? Mother always called them that," added Tamara.

"Yes, the same," responded Father. "Now, to continue your indoctrination: The air is replaced by drawing upon the oxygen that is found in water. We can live comfortably within the palace without having to depend on our gills. The interior walls are made from crushed seashells, sand and lava."

"Lava! How can those three materials combine to make walls?" she asked.

"Many things were possible when the Sisters were working as one. There is an undersea volcano not too far from here that was the source of the molten lava. White magic was used to form the walls from those sources," said Father.

"What happened between the Sisters?" asked Tamara. "Why are they no longer friends?"

"As you know, the four Super Siblings have been around for many of our generations. While they have taken lovers, they have never married any mortals. This state of equilibrium suddenly changed when the two Sisters both fell in love with my father. He was a strikingly handsome man and very charming. When the time came for him to marry, he chose Solange over Savea. Savea was both hurt and angry, blaming Solange for everything. She moved to the volcano and began sending fire balls toward the palace. Solange erected a force field to repel that fire magic. Unfortunately, that rift between the Sisters has never healed."

Tamara was stunned. "So Solange is your mother?" she asked.

"That's right," her father replied.

"Do you have powers then, Father?"

"That is unknown. Until you were born, I believed that I was unique among mortals since I was an only child. But now…you certainly must be aware that you are different from your friends? I believe that you have indeed inherited powers from Solange, through me, although they seem to be just coming to the surface."

Tamara grabbed her father's arm. "You're serious!" she

cried. "I've always known about my crystal, but it just sat there on my stomach and I almost forgot about it—until today when it started to glow! I'm so confused! What is happening to me? I asked mother and she didn't know."

"Speaking of your mother, we are near the infirmary and you can see her and your sister—but just for a few minutes."

They came to a double door and pushed it open. There were eight beds in the room, but only two beds were presently occupied. Tamara rushed over to the bed where her mother lay sleeping. "Mother," she cried, "Please wake up!"

But her mother didn't stir. She lay still, her face pale against the pillowcase. Tamara turned to the other bed where her sister Trina rested. "Trina, it's me, Tamara. Please open your eyes."

"Tamara," said Father, "We have to let them rest. If either one awakens, the nurse will call us. Come with me now. I'd like to introduce you to your grandmother."

Chapter 3
Meeting Solange

They reentered the corridor and walked toward a flight of stairs. Climbing to the next floor, they walked to a door carved of silver and decorated with images of dolphins. Using the seashell door knocker, they rapped three times. The door swung open and a young girl dressed in a short silver dress welcomed them into the room. "Her Highness, Solange, is resting, but I will let her know that you are here, Your Majesty," she said demurely. "Please make yourselves comfortable." Turning away, she walked toward an ornate silver door on the back wall and entered another room, closing the door behind her.

"Your Majesty?" gasped Tamara. "Mother had told me that you returned to the sea because your father was ill. Did he die, Father?"

"Yes, Tamara. That's why I couldn't return to the land. My duty to the kingdom prevented it. I love you, your mother and sister very much. Please sit next to me on the sofa."

"But couldn't you have let us know?" Tamara asked as she lowered herself onto the silver and aquamarine plaid sofa.

"Mother looked out to sea every day, hoping that she

would see you coming home."

"I wanted to," replied Father. "Terra, your mother, understood why I had to leave. Please understand that time has a different meaning beneath the sea. On land, time is governed by a period of day followed by a period of night and it is easy to measure the passage of time. Here, time has no similar parameters and, while we do have waking and sleeping times, there is no overall pattern of time distribution. Therefore, even though I had every intention of sending word to your mother, the combination of duty and fluidity of time made sending that message a lesser priority. Now that I see how grown up you are, I deeply regret that delay. We've missed out on so much."

"And it took a tsunami to bring us together," cried Tamara. "I suppose I should be grateful for that."

"It was definitely a mixed blessing," her father said with a sad smile. "I'm still hopeful that your mother and sister will awaken soon."

The silver door suddenly opened and a beautiful woman who looked not much older than Tamara came swiftly toward them. She was wearing a silver brocade gown embellished with golden embroidered dolphins and a crown of black pearls on her head. Her silver hair fell in a long cascade down her back. Her silver eyes were wet with tears as she held out both hands to Tamara and cried, "You must be Tamara! You look so much like your father!"

Rising from the sofa, Tamara gazed in awe at this stunning creature who certainly did not look like any grandmother she had ever seen. Coming to her rescue, her father said, "Yes, Mother, this is Tamara. I am so pleased that you are able to meet at last."

Tamara and her father returned to the sofa while Solange chose an adjoining chair upholstered in aquamarine velvet. Looking at Tamara, she said, "I'm sure you have many questions. Your arrival here was sudden and unanticipated by anyone, including yourself. How can I help you with your concerns?"

Looking at her hands, Tamara thought for a moment and then looked into Solange's silver eyes. "Yes, I do have questions. Most of them can be combined into one: Who am I and why am I different from everyone else I know? Until I came here and found my father, of course."

"That's really two questions, but they are certainly connected. I understand that you were not aware of our relationship. Your mother didn't know either, of course. We didn't intend secrecy; it's just that having a magical super being for a mother-in-law would be more than a little daunting, so I kept a low profile."

"So mother never knew? She was so confused when

father left and never came back."

"That was due to an unfortunate set of circumstances," replied Solange. "After your father left the land because of my husband's illness, there was so little time before death claimed him and forced your father to assume the throne. It was not what we would have wished, but fate has a way of re-ordering lives."

Tamara rose and walked across the room to a mirror. "And it seems that fate is now re-ordering mine. I no longer have a home on land and my mother and sister may never awaken. I have a crystal on my stomach and, while none of my friends or family have one, it seems to have come alive and is constantly changing colors—along with my hair!" Tears began to slide down her cheeks as she looked sadly at her reflected image

Solange moved quickly to her side and held her tenderly. "I understand that the world that you knew has been turned upside down, my dear. Come and sit beside me on the sofa and I'll try to explain about your crystal."

Slowly they strolled back to the sofa and sat facing each other as her father moved over to the door. "I think you two need a little get-acquainted time. I'll be in my office downstairs. Please come there when you are finished." He smiled and closed the door behind him.

Tamara turned to Solange and sighed, "Not every girl has

a magical grandmother, I guess. I'll try to get used to it, but you don't look much older than me."

"I can see that my appearance would not be that of a typical grandmother. Remember that I age very slowly."

"How old are you?" asked Tamara.

"I've lost track, but I have lived through many generations of land and sea dwellers. I should add that having such a young looking mother has also been problematic for your father as he has grown older, even though he does age more slowly than his peers."

"I can imagine! But isn't it going to be hard on you to outlive your son eventually? And how long do you think your life will be?

"I don't know. But I expect that it will be many, many years. But let's talk about you. Your father tells me that you were born with a crystal on your stomach. Tell me about it."

Tamara hesitated and then said, "I've always had it, I guess. My mother told me that father foretold that I would become important to the Marinean people—but I don't know how. My crystal has always just been there—until my last birthday. I woke up that morning and it was glowing! I ran to mother's bedroom and asked her what was happening, but she didn't know. She did tell me to stay home from school and we would watch it. The next moment, the crystal turned yellow—

and so did my hair! Mother teased me about always wanting to be a blonde like my sister."

"So let me fully understand. The crystal was quiet until your seventeenth birthday, when it began to glow and then it turned yellow. Is this correct so far?"

"Yes. But there is more. I went down to the ocean to walk on the beach. I was splashing in the water when a few strands of hair blew across my face—and it was green! I checked my crystal and it was green, too."

"Ah," said Solange. "I'm beginning to understand. There is a pattern here."

"What do you mean?"

"When the earthquake struck, did you notice the color of your crystal and your hair?" asked Solange.

"Yes, they had turned yellow again," answered Tamara.

"That makes sense," commented Solange. "Here's what I think is happening. First of all, your hormones are increasingly active because of your age. Did your mother mention that you are coming of age?"

"She told me that on my tenth birthday, but I didn't notice any changes."

"That's good information, too," said Solange. "Your life pattern and length of years may be extraordinary, somewhat like mine. We shall have to think about that. But first, let's return to the colors that you experience in your crystal and your hair. Here is my theory: Your hormones have a strong influence on your emotions—which run hot and intense at your time of life. I'm going to guess that yellow is the reflection of fear. Yellow occurred when you first discovered that the crystal was glowing and also when you felt the quake. Green is probably an indication of peacefulness or contentment—like when you were walking the beach and playing in the surf. Does this sound reasonable?"

"Yes, I think so. What a fun idea! I change colors like the rainbow!"

"Not exactly," Solange replied. "But your emotional state would be pretty obvious to everyone. I think we are going to need to work on self-discipline and the centering of your spirit so that you can learn to control your emotions—and your colors."

Tamara hugged her grandmother and said, "I'm so happy to have an explanation for what's been happening to me! And I'd love to learn how to manage my colors."

Solange and Tamara walked arm in arm toward the door. "Let's go and find your father," Solange suggested. "And then we need to find your bedroom and settle you in."

Chapter 4
Lessons

The next morning, Tamara woke with a start, not knowing where she was. Looking around the room, she thought, I'm back in that blue-green room that I was in yesterday. This must be my bedroom. She decided to take a shower and dress for the day, hoping that it really was day. It felt very strange to know that she was underwater and that the normal division of day and night was not readily apparent. She walked toward the bath area and stepped behind the screen. There was a sink area decorated with seashells and a large bathtub against the wall. Facing the tub, she gasped with delight. Over the tub was a large circular skylight and she could see fish swimming just like an aquarium—except that it was the outside ocean that she was viewing. *"How magnificent!"* she thought.

There were two faucet handles at one end of the tub. Carefully checking water temperature, she filled the tub with water. She lay back in the tub and watched the swimming fish and feeling the warm water lull her into a marvelous state of relaxation.

After bathing, she returned to the bedroom and approached the clothing cabinet. *"Hmm,"* she mused. *"I think I'll wear this long blue and silver gown. It looks so soft and comfortable."*

There was a soft knock at the door and Mia entered. "Is there anything that I can do for you this morning?" Mia asked.

"Oh good, then it IS morning," replied Tamara. "How does one tell?"

Mia explained, "You can observe the skylight over your bath: in the day, the fish are easy to sea and the water is very blue; at night, many fish sleep and the water is quite dark. Another way is to touch this panel by the door, which will give you the date, day and time. Your father had it installed to help you adjust."

"That seems easy enough. Thank you so much for telling me," exclaimed Tamara. "Is it time for breakfast?"

"Yes," answered Mia. "Your father awaits you in the breakfast room."

* * * * *

"Good morning, Father. Good morning, Grandmother," said Tamara, taking her seat at the breakfast table. This room was smaller and more intimate than the formal dining room of the night before. A series of skylight views of the ocean brought light into the room. Fish of many colors swam lazily overhead. The walls and floor were covered with tiles in various shades of blue. Soft music echoed throughout the room. The table was laden with a variety of breakfast options, including turtle eggs, seaweed bread, and fish cakes.

"Did you sleep well, my dear?" asked her father.

"Yes, Father, thank you. But I was very disoriented when I awakened. I didn't know where I was."

"That's not surprising," Solange commented. "You have had a traumatic couple of days. Trident, do you need Tamara for anything today? If not, I think we should begin her lessons."

"Trident?" asked Tamara. "Is that your given name, Father?"

"Yes, Tamara," replied her father. "I was named for a god of the sea. It seems fitting, somehow. And no, Mother, I don't have any plans for Tamara today. I think that beginning her lessons would be a good idea. But first, let's enjoy our breakfast."

Tamara selected fish cakes and bread, with a side of berries. "Father, I understand that most of the food choices come from the sea, but where do the berries come from?"

"We have a hydroponic garden adjacent to the palace where many foods that you would recognize from the land are grown. Your meals will have a nice variety of options. Things won't seem so strange after a while."

"I like the sound of that!" Tamara laughed. She decided

that she was really hungry and attacked her breakfast with enthusiasm. "Does that garden supply food to all of the Marineans?"

"No," replied Father. "There are hydroponic gardens scattered all across the kingdom. One garden couldn't possibly produce sufficient quantities to feed everyone."

"Someday, will you take me on a tour of your kingdom, Father?" asked Tamara.

"I'd be delighted, my dear. Perhaps in a few days."

After the dishes had been cleared away, Tamara asked, "Before we start my lessons, could I visit mother and Trina?"

"Of course, dear," responded Solange. Let's see if there is any change in their condition."

Walking down the corridor to the infirmary, Tamara and Solange linked arms. Tamara asked, "Grandmother, do you think mother and Trina will regain consciousness? And will they get well?"

"I don't know, my dear. But I certainly hope so."

"Can't you use your magic to help them?" asked Tamara. "Mother told me that you have great powers that you use for good purposes."

"Both your father and I combined our magic to save them from the tsunami," replied Solange. "We rushed to their side and encased them in a bubble of air. This is why they survived the disaster. Now we have to wait and see if their will to live is strong enough. Meanwhile, remember that they are resting comfortably and are sustaining no further injuries."

"I'm just so afraid for them," cried Tamara. "I don't know what I would do if anything happened to either of them."

"Don't worry, my dear. I think everything will turn out just fine. But have you noticed that your hair is totally yellow again? How are you feeling right now?"

"I'm fearful and worried, and a little sad," replied Tamara.

"Sadness must mean blue, since your hair is showing some streaks of that color."

"Oh my! I guess you're right about the connection between my emotions and my colors."

"I believe so."

Pushing open the door of the Infirmary, they walked over to the two occupied beds. There didn't seem to be any change in the condition of Tamara's mother and sister. Both of them slept peacefully and the machines monitoring their vital signs beeped quietly.

Tamara leaned over and kissed her mother's brow. Her mother sighed, her eyelids fluttered, and then she returned to a deep sleep. "I love you, Mother. We're doing everything we can to make you better," Tamara promised. Moving over to her sister's bed, she took her hand and pressed it gently.

"Trina, can you hear me? Please wake up," she pleaded. But there was no response. Sadly, she walked back to the door.

Solange put her arm around Tamara's shoulders. "They are holding their own," she said. "Please calm yourself. We have a Meditation Chapel here in the palace. Let's go there and begin your lessons."

A few minutes later, they had arrived at a mirrored door and entered the Chapel. Soft cushions were scattered across the glass floor and candles were placed at strategic locations throughout the room. Solange clapped her hands and the candles burst into flame while strains of peaceful music filled the air. The candlelight reflected on the glass walls of the Chapel.

Tamara looked around and exclaimed, "The walls seem to shimmer and change color!"

"Yes, but much more will happen as you learn to control your thoughts and feelings," explained Solange. "Think about the earthquake and see what occurs."

Tamara pressed her fingers to her temples and the glass walls seemed to ripple and shake. The music became atonal and frantic as her memories brought back the terror of the quake. The walls began to show scenes of what Tamara was remembering, magnifying the sensation of what she was reliving. Her crystal and her hair were glowing bright yellow.

Tears began to flow down her cheeks and she cried, "How do I stop this?"

Solange took her hand and led her to one of the cushions. "Sit quietly and close your eyes. Breathe deeply. Think about your birthday walk on the beach. Listen to the surf and the birds, feel the sun upon your face, and splash in the water."

Tamara lay back on the cushion and tried to relax. Slowly, her deepening breaths resulted in a change of hair color from yellow to blue.

"Good," said Solange. "It's working. How do you feel now?"

"Much better. And my crystal and hair are blue! Is that the goal: to keep my hair blue?"

"Actually, that would be a good beginning. Our ultimate goal, however, is to keep your hair white without changing color. That would mean that you are totally centered and in control of your responses to outside influences."

"Why is that important, Grandmother?" asked Tamara.

"Because you need to keep your thoughts and emotions under control and not visible to others if you are to rule one day," replied Solange.

"Rule! What do you mean?"

"You are Trident's oldest child and heir presumptive to the throne. It is fortunate that you have inherited Marinean characteristics, such as gills. That will make you more acceptable to our people."

"This is amazing!" cried Tamara. "And overwhelming!"

"I'm sure it is hard to absorb all at once," replied Solange. "So let's approach it a little at a time. For the next hour, I'm going to ask you to relive different memories. As before, I want you to substitute a pleasant memory for one that is upsetting. We will practice this exercise over and over until you can sufficiently exert your will to be in command of the situation. Now let us begin…"

Chapter 5
The Great Awakening

Several weeks later, Tamara and Solange were finishing a morning's lesson and preparing to leave for lunch. They were strolling past the Infirmary when Tamara impulsively suggested that they stop briefly to see her mother and sister. Entering the Infirmary, Tamara hurried to her mother's bedside.

"Mother, it's Tamara," she said.

Solange suggested that she continue talking since her mother's eyes had been fluttering in response during past visits.

"Please wake up," urged Tamara. "I miss you so much. It's really wonderful here under the sea and I know that you would love it."

Holding her mother's hand, she bent to kiss her cheek. Suddenly, she felt the gentle touch of eyelashes on her brow and exclaimed. "Mother, can you hear me?"

A soft sigh came from her mother's lips and she squeezed Tamara's fingers. "Where am I," she asked.

"Mother! You're awake!" Tamara cried, throwing her arms around her, looking over at Solange with tears in her eyes.

Solange rushed to her side and said, with a broad smile, "I'll get your father."

Once Solange had left the Infirmary, Tamara carefully raised the bed beneath her mother's head. Opening her eyes, her mother gazed lovingly at Tamara and asked, "What happened? What day is it?"

"You've been asleep for weeks, Mother. Do you remember the earthquake? A huge sinkhole opened under our cottage and swallowed it. Solange and Father rescued you and brought you here to his palace. We're under the sea."

"Oh my," her mother replied. "What an adventure you've had! Where is Trina? Is she OK?"

"She's right over there in the next bed. She hasn't awakened yet."

"Help me get up. I need to go to her."

Tamara helped her mother swing her legs over the side of the bed. Standing tentatively, she held on to Tamara's arm and walked to her younger daughter's bedside. "Trina, darling. Please wake up."

Stroking Trina's hair, Tamara looked at her mother and explained that there had been no sign that Trina was even aware of their presence. They turned to each other and hugged silently, tears spilling from their eyes. Suddenly the room began to shake and a vase of flowers on a side table crashed to the floor. There was a loud rumble and Tamara covered her ears. Trina's bed slid toward the far wall and she sat up screaming, "Mother! Earthquake! Help!"

Tamara and her mother ran to the bed and tried to halt its slide. "Trina, you're awake!" cried Tamara. Sobbing, Trina flung herself into her mother's arms. Just then, the infirmary door burst open and Tamara's father and Solange ran into the room.

"Is everyone all right?" Solange asked.

"We're fine, and the quake woke Trina," Tamara explained.

"That's really good news," said Trident, taking Terra in his arms. "I'm so relieved that you are both back with us from your extended sleep."

"Father, what caused the quake?" asked Tamara.

Trident looked worriedly at Solange and replied, "We haven't had a quake since the one that caused the sinkhole, and no quakes for many years before then. Your grandmother and I have been trying to understand what is happening and we have a theory"

Solange elaborated, "My sister has been living near an undersea volcano ever since we had that falling out when I married your grandfather. At that time, she was so angry that we had many quakes, but she has quieted down over time. I believe that she sensed your coming of age, Tamara, and the power that accompanies that development. That probably brought all those old feelings to the surface and she is becoming active again."

"What does that mean, Grandmother?" asked Tamara. "What is she likely to do? And what will happen to us?"

"My sister is a very powerful Being," Solange explained. "Her anger is something to be feared and I think that we should help you to return to Alteria."

Trident agreed, "That would also be my recommendation. We can take the Bubble Train to the stop close to Alteria and then swim to land. It has been some time since I have been on land and, when I lived with you there, I had no official role to play on behalf of Marinea. It is time that I establish diplomatic relations with the Council of Elders of Alteria. I will accompany you on your journey and meet with the Council."

"What's a Bubble Train, Father?" asked Tamara.

"It's a train that has air bubbles instead of regular cars and is one of our major means of transportation. When we leave the train, I will see that your mother and sister have rebreathers so that they can swim comfortably to shore. You, of course, now have gills and can swim on your own.

"Solange, would you please send a message to the Council by way of a postal seagull and let them know I am coming.

"Seagull?" queried Tamara. "Seagulls take messages? I've heard that carrier pigeons do, but never seagulls."

"Specially trained postal gulls are very good messengers," replied her father. "But I think the Council Elders may never have encountered one before and may be quite surprised."

"How long do the three of you need to pack your things?" asked Solange.

"Not long," replied Terra. "Trina and I really don't have anything of our own here. But I have concerns. Once we reach Alteria, I don't know what to do."

Trident suggested that they travel with him to the capital city of Newmarin and visit Terra's sister and her family. "I'm sure she would be delighted to see you and know that you are safe. I'll do whatever I can to help you find your own quarters. Of course, you are welcome to remain here in the palace but, until we figure out what to do about Savea and her anger, I think it will be safer for you on land."

"Mother, Trina, I'm so happy that you are awake and well. It's hard for me to say this since we have all just been reunited, but I think I should stay here with Solange," said Tamara. "We have recently begun some important lessons and I think I should continue."

"But won't you be in danger?" asked her mother.

Solange responded, "We would be together and my

powers are as strong as my sister's. Remember that we were once one Being until our parents decided to split our essence into two. Please don't worry. Trident, what do you think?"

"Tamara should be fine. And she will be good company for you, Mother."

Solange put her arm around Tamara's shoulders. "That's settled, then. When will you leave?"

"Within the hour. I have some papers to gather and it won't take long to pack. Terra, Trina, is that acceptable to you?"

"Yes, Trident," answered Terra. "Where shall we meet you?"

"Downstairs in the palace foyer. Shall we say in 45 minutes?"

"That sounds fine. Trina, let's freshen up and do our packing," suggested Terra, taking her younger daughter's arm and walking to the door. "Tamara, will you come and say goodbye before we leave?"

"Of course, Mother. I'll come to your room in a few minutes," Tamara responded as she sat on the sofa.

"Grandmother, please come and sit by me. I have some questions to ask you.

"You mentioned that you and Savea were once one Being. I've always thought that was a legend. But then so many things that I've assumed were stories are turning out to be true."

Solange paused a moment, looking up through the skylight at the fish swimming overhead. "I can understand your confusion. These things are not easy to understand. My parents are very powerful Beings and they feared that their two original offspring might become too strong for them to control. By splitting our essences, our individual power was reduced and they felt more secure. But each of us was left feeling as if there is something missing in our lives. Our essences yearn to be reunited.

"So it was no surprise that both Savea and I fell in love with your grandfather. The sad part is that there were two of us and only one of him, so he had to choose. Once he chose me, Savea's dark spirit became enraged and she fled the palace, taking shelter in that undersea volcano. When she is upset, she causes tremors and spurts lava flows. Her anger has never abated. These current upheavals are a result of her awareness that you are receiving your powers. She feels a change in the power relationship between us and is fearful.

"We haven't spoken since my wedding day, and you know how long ago that was. But, like many sets of human twins, we do sense each other and often are aware of the other's feelings and thoughts. With this increase in volcanic and thermal activity, I think it's important that I try to contact her."

"I'd like to help you, Grandmother," said Tamara.

"Especially since I seem to be the cause of her current emotional displays."

Solange paced back and forth, a look of intense concentration on her face. "I think that's an idea worth considering. Let's continue to talk about it, but in the meantime we must continue your lessons so that you can learn to effectively harness your emerging powers."

"Yes, Grandmother," agreed Tamara, "but first, I promised to say goodbye to Mother and Trina in their room. Will you be coming or shall I meet you in the foyer?"

"The foyer will be fine. Then you can also bid farewell to your father."

Tamara crossed over to the door and entered the hall. Moving quickly, she arrived at her mother's bedroom and knocked softly. "Mother, may I come in?" she asked.

Terra opened the door and drew her daughter inside. "I'm worried," she sighed. "I do understand that we must leave since I have no powers to defend us and it's too soon to tell about Trina, but what will become of you? You haven't had time to fully explore your powers with Solange."

"That's true," Tamara replied. "But we will be continuing to work on that and please remember that Solange is as powerful as her sister. I will be fine, Mother. Look I've already learned to control the colors of my crystal and my hair."

"I'm very impressed," said her mother. "I've never told you, but the day you were born, there was a small whirlwind right there in the room with me. Objects in the room were flying everywhere and the doctor had all he could handle with the delivery. When the wind ceased and you were placed in my arms, there was a crystal on your stomach. Everyone was amazed."

"Really! I'm so glad you told me. I'll discuss it with Solange and see if she can interpret the meaning of that experience. Meanwhile, are you and Trina finished packing and ready to go downstairs?"

"Yes, we are," said Trina.

Tamara hugged her mother and sister and they all descended to the foyer where Solange and Triton were waiting for them. Triton motioned to a nearby hallway. "The Bubble Train has a station here in the palace. It's only a short walk."

"How convenient!" exclaimed Terra. "I'm very impressed. But remember to show us how that rebreather works so we are ready when it's time to leave the train."

"Don't worry. I'll be there with you," said Triton. As they all walked to the train, the floor began to undulate and Terra grabbed Triton's arm. "What is happening?" she cried.

Solange replied, "My sister is expressing her displeasure. We must hurry." They started to run and soon arrived at the station. The Bubble Train awaited them.

With quick hugs all around, Triton, Terra and Trina boarded the train and were soon gone from sight. The tremors continued and Solange and Tamara cautiously made their way back to the foyer. "I think it would be a good idea to return to the Meditation Chapel," recommended Solange. "I need to focus my thoughts in order to contact my sister."

Climbing the stairs, they carefully made their way to the Chapel. Once inside, they chose chairs across from each other and held hands. Closing their eyes, they attempted to center their spirits. If an observer had been present, she would have noticed a glow starting to surround their bodies, rivaling the soft lighting emanating from the walls around them. The glow became more brilliant over Solange and started to pulsate, becoming rhythmic and alternating between aquamarine and red tones. Tamara opened her eyes and stared in wonder.

Her grandmother's face was strained with effort and concentration.

Suddenly, a cloud became visible in the room and slowly turned into the figure of a woman dressed in a long, flowing red garment. Her hair was black and her dark eyes were full of fury. "Who summons me?" she cried.

"I did," answered Solange. "We need to talk."

"I see nothing to discuss with You," hissed Savea.

"But there is," Solange insisted. "You are very angry and have been so for a very long time. I had hoped that as the years passed, your resentment would have lessened. But this hasn't happened. What can I do to bring peace to your heart?"

"Peace!" exclaimed Savea. "You stole the love of my life and expect me to forget? That will never happen!"

"These bad feelings are eating away at your spirit," pleaded Solange. "You are my sister and we were once one Being. My husband and your love is no more. Can we not now mend the rift between us?" Solange held out her arms to Savea as tears fell from her eyes. "Sister, please!"

A cloud began to form and swirl around Savea as she prepared to leave in the same manner that she arrived. Tamara's eyes were moist as she suddenly moved forward and reached for Savea's hand, pulling her from the cloud. She clasped the hands of both Sisters and the room filled with a white light. The three women fell to the floor unconscious.

* * * * *

Soft music was playing as Tamara began to stir. Slowly sitting up, she noticed that the candles on the Chapel's altar had burned down significantly and were almost ready to go out. She looked around the room and saw Solange and Savea still lying insensible on the floor. She crawled over to her grandmother and tried unsuccessfully to rouse her. Turning to Savea, she shook her shoulder and received no response. *"Oh my,"* she worried. *"What has happened and why won't they awaken?"*

Noticing a small fountain in the corner of the Chapel, she hurried over and dipped her scarf in the cool water. Returning to her grandmother, she placed the damp cloth on her forehead as she pleaded, "Grandmother, please wake up!" Wryly, she realized that she had been saying those same words a lot lately.

Solange moaned and her eyelids fluttered. "Tamara, how did I get on the floor?"

"I don't know. When I touched your hands and Savea's hands, there was a bright light and that's all I remember."

Another moan caught their attention and they looked over at Savea, who was beginning to move into a sitting position. "Wow! That was interesting. Solange, are you all right?"

"I'm fine. Did you just call me by my name?"

"Of course I did," replied Savea.

"You haven't used my given name since I was married," explained Solange.

"Really?" wondered Savea. "I do somehow remember being angry with you—I guess for a long time. But I don't feel that way anymore."

Solange rushed to her sister's side and they embraced

tearfully. "I don't know what has softened your heart and mended the rift between us, but I am so happy."

Solange stiffened. Her eyes rolled upward and she whispered, "The Bubble Train...the Bubble Train..."

Tamara asked, "Has my family arrived at land, or are they still on board the train?" Her face lost its color. "Suddenly, I'm very frightened!"

"I'm afraid they might still be enroute," worried Solange. "I'll try to link to your father's mind to see if they are safe."

Solange sat quietly and a golden glow surrounded her. Tamara and Savea watched her closely and then cried out as the glow turned into an aura of fire. "Grandmother, what is happening?" Tamara screamed.

The fire flared and then subsided as Solange fainted again.

Chapter 6
A New Order

The soft illumination of the walls of the Chapel seemed to blend in with the sound of peaceful music. Solange slowly opened her eyes as Tamara again placed a cool cloth on her forehead. "Grandmother, are you all right?" she asked.

Reaching out her arms to hold her granddaughter, Solange could not speak. Tears soaked Tamara's shoulder as Solange cried and cried. The two women held each other tightly until the sobs subsided. Savea put her arms around them and gently tried to soothe her sister and grandniece. After some time, Solange held Tamara at arm's length and said softly, "They're gone. The Bubble Train was derailed by an intense red beam and an eruption of lava. I felt the impact…and then, nothing. I don't think anyone survived."

"What! My whole family has been destroyed? And just when I've found my father again? cried Tamara helplessly. "How? When? Who?"

Solange stood and walked slowly across the room. "I don't know. We are certain of one thing: Savea was not responsible."

"Me? Of course not! I wouldn't do anything to harm them."

"But you would have, just a few hours ago. Remember how you were ranting before that bright light felled us?"

"You're right. I might have done something foolish. I'm so sorry and, while I don't understand it, I'm grateful to that light."

"But then who?" asked Tamara tearfully. "Who would want my family dead?"

Solange thought for a minute, her brow furrowed, and glancing over at Savea replied, "We need to think carefully about that and plan our strategy for your future."

Leaping up and running toward her grandmother, Tamara grabbed Solange's hands and sank to her knees. "What do you mean—MY future? I'm an orphan. I have no future!"

Solange knelt beside Tamara and said softly, "I told you before that you were the heir to the kingdom. I don't think that you really understood the ramifications of what I said. At that time, I believed that we had a lot of time to prepare you for this responsibility. Sadly, Fate has once again re-ordered our lives and you are now faced with immediate succession to the throne."

Tamara shook her head and looked despairingly at the two Sisters. "How can you ask this of me? I've just lost my entire family. I don't know how I can endure."

"I know that you are broken-hearted, my child." murmured

Solange. "But you are also strong and resilient. It is unfortunate that we were deprived of the opportunity to explore your powers at a leisurely pace and that your future has been rewritten so suddenly. We will take a brief time to grieve together…you haven't lost all your family for Savea and I are here…and then we must move forward."

"But Grandmother, I don't know if I can. My spirit feels bruised and broken."

"Yes, that seems obvious," said Solange dryly. "Your hair is black now. We really must increase those centering exercises so that you can learn to control those strong emotions of yours.

Solange gently lifted Tamara to her feet and said, "Let's just live from moment to moment for today. I'll walk you to your bedroom while Savea sees to some refreshment for us. It is absolutely necessary to eat well in order to maintain health and strength. Tomorrow we will begin to plan and strategize, but tonight is for tears and remembering. Savea, would you please ask Mia to bring some tea and biscuits to Tamara's room?"

* * * * *

A light tap at the bedroom door woke Tamara from a night of turbulent dreams. Reaching for her robe, she padded over to the door and asked, "Who is it?"

"It's Mia, Your Highness," came the reply. "I've brought you your breakfast." Opening the door, Tamara gestured to Mia to enter and place the tray on a nearby table. "Thank you, Mia," she murmured as Mia curtseyed and left the room. Staring down at the plate of crab cakes, seaweed bread and jam, she wondered how she would ever eat anything since her stomach was churning and her eyes brimmed with unshed tears. Perhaps I can calm my insides with a cup of tea, she thought, pouring from a lovely pot covered with images of shells.

Sitting quietly, she sipped her tea and looked around the room. Spotting a vid-screen on the far wall, she reached for a control wand and turned on the ANN network for the latest news. Stunned, she watched an account of the results of the Bubble Train disaster, which was reported in an atmosphere of confusion since no land dweller had ever seen a Bubble Train… and no one could determine where the bodies came from, since there was no boat in the area. The announcer commented that there was considerable burn damage of unknown origin. The bodies had been transported to the local morgue for autopsies and notification of next-of-kin.

Tamara sighed and turned off the screen. She wondered how she would be able to return to Alteria to claim the bodies of her beloved family and make final arrangements. There would be so many questions and how would she be able to answer them? Picking gingerly at her breakfast, she decided that she would have to speak as soon as possible to Solange about this.

Another knock at the door and Solange entered the room. "Ah, you are at breakfast. Shall I come back later?" she asked.

"No, please sit down," replied Tamara. "I need to talk to you about the arrangements for my family."

"Of course," Solange said. "There will be complications, of course."

"Why, what do you mean? Asked Tamara.

"It is not safe for you to leave here at this time. We don't yet know if that lava eruption was a coincidence or was caused by someone. Didn't your mother have a land-based sister?"

"Yes. Mother and Trina planned to stay with her while Father established his diplomatic and ambassadorial credentials."

"Did your aunt know they were coming?" asked Solange.

"I believe so," replied Tamara.

"Then I think it would be best to send her a carrier seagull, explaining the situation and asking her to take control of the arrangements. I know it will be very painful for you not to be there, but we need to take a longer view."

"But Grandmother, surely I need to be at the funeral?"

" We'll ask your aunt to make a video for you and we'll hold a memorial service here," suggested Solange. "You must realize that you are in danger and would be entirely too vulnerable if you were to try and reach the land at this time. We must move quickly to prepare for your coronation and make decisions about how to handle Savea."

Tamara wept softly, but reluctantly agreed to Solange's plans.

*   *   *   *   *

Later that morning, the two grieving women met in the library to begin talking about the future. Curling up on a comfortable sofa, they were silent for a few minutes while they pondered how to begin.

Solange broke the silence first. "I think that we should first contact your aunt and alert her to what is needed. We will have to include instructions on how to communicate with us. I hope that she will agree to keep our conversations—and our existence-- confidential. If she doesn't, we shall have to deal with that later."

Tamara nodded her head. "I think that's the best place to start. I trust that she will do so. I met her a couple of times while I was growing up and she seemed very nice."

"Meanwhile," added Solange, "We must begin the

preparations for your coronation. Our kingdom must have a ruler. I suggest we aim for a simple, yet elegant, ceremony in one week's time. Do you agree?"

"Oh my goodness! So soon?" asked Tamara.

"Yes. We must create stability in this time of crisis," replied Solange. "Be courageous, my dear. I know you can do this. Have you heard from your aunt?"

"Yes. There was a memorial service on Alteria. She said it was very well attended. I'd like to have one here as well, as soon as possible."

"Of course, my dear. We'll arrange it for just following your coronation."

"All right, Grandmother. I will do my best not to disappoint you."

"Good. I will contact the necessary people to help us with the ceremony. In the meantime, why don't you practice your centering exercises? Your hair is quite yellow at the moment."

*   *   *   *   *

One week later, Tamara gazed at her reflection in the mirror and thought about how this day would unfold. In a few minutes, someone would come to escort her to the Ballroom for her coronation as Queen of Marinea. She was still reeling from the sudden deaths of her family and, without a single pause it seemed, she was being groomed to be a monarch. It was a daunting thought and she hoped that she would be able to become the Queen that the kingdom needed.

Her image in the mirror stared back at her. At least those centering exercises have had an effect, she thought, as she marveled at her white hair. *"No sign of emotion. Good."*

She did a slow pirouette in the new gown that had been fashioned especially for the ceremony. It was an iridescent aqua blue fabric encrusted with pearls. A strand of exquisite matched pearls circled her slender neck with matching earrings as her only additional jewelry. Her thoughts were in a turmoil. She sorely missed her parents and sister and was fearful of the overwhelming responsibility that she was about to assume. She paced back and forth nervously and almost didn't hear the tapping at her door.

Hurrying to the door, she found her grandmother dressed in a gown worthy of the rank of Queen Mother/Grandmother. "You look beautiful!" they said simultaneously. Laughing, they linked arms and began to walk toward the Ballroom. All at once they stopped and stared at the woman walking toward them.

" Grandmother, isn't that Savea?" asked Tamara."I thought she had left the palace."

"Indeed it is…and she's dressed for the ceremony!"

Drawing closer, they came face to face with Savea. "Hello, Savea," said Solange.

"I've come to pay my respects to our new Queen. I'm sorry that I've been absent since that extraordinary night with the bright light, but I've had some affairs to attend to."

"Have you found out anything as to what might have been the cause of the train disaster?" Solange asked Savea.

"That's why I returned home. Since I live near a volcano, I have certain knowledge of tectonic movements and lava flows. I used my powers to explore all the lava tubes and eruption locations between Marinea and Alteria and found nothing out of the ordinary—except for the isolated incident that destroyed the Bubble Train. I have to conclude that more than natural forces were in play here. I'm afraid that I can't identify the cause—not yet. But we do need to find out. That, however, is our mission for tomorrow. Today is Tamara's day and we have a coronation to attend," said Savea.

"Savea, I have to ask: Why are you being so nice?" Tamara pressed. "You've been feuding with Solange for years and you haven't played any part in my life before now. Why the change of heart?"

" You ask good questions. I guess my temper tantrum served as a much needed venting for the emotions that had been building inside me for such a long time…and then there was that light, of course. I hope you both can forgive me."

Tamara looked at Solange and asked, "Do you believe her? Is she sincere?"

Solange stood quietly for a moment and then clasped Savea's hands. They held their positions for several minutes as a golden glow surrounded them. Finally, they stepped apart and Solange said, "Yes, she is being truthful. Remember that we were once one Being and I can tune in on her thoughts and feelings."

"And she really didn't have anything to do with killing my family?" asked Tamara.

"That's right," replied Solange. "There is some other explanation and we will find it—starting tomorrow. Now, let's walk together to the Ballroom. I can hardly wait to see the looks on the faces of our citizens when they see Savea!"

Chapter 7
Tamara's Powers

Stretching like a lazy cat, Tamara opened one eye and then looked around her room. Sitting abruptly up in bed, she thought, "*Oh my, I'm the Queen!* "Smiling, she remembered the festivities of the day before: the coronation ceremony, the surprise of Savea's appearance, the outpouring of love and good will from everyone present. It was a truly special day and one she would never forget.

She swung her legs to the floor and shoved her feet into slippers. Hurrying to the wardrobe, she selected a dress in a soft blue velvet, hoping that it would make her look appropriately regal. Searching for some suitable jewelry, she decided on a gold pendant and chain with matching earrings. Reaching for her hairbrush, her hands clinked against the handle. Gazing at her palms, she was startled. Shining crystals caught the light. Bemused, she brushed her long white hair briskly—thankfully, it was still white—and was about to leave for the breakfast room when she heard a knock at the door.

"Enter," she said. The door slowly opened and Savea entered. "Do you have a minute to talk?"

"Certainly. Have you had breakfast?"

"Yes, but I don't want to keep you from yours."

"Breakfast can wait. What can I do for you, Savea?"

"I have a theory about the Bubble Train tragedy. But it's only a theory."

"Go on…"

"You know that Solange and I have two Brothers: Sostor and Sunan. Sostor controls ice magic on the north mainland and Sunan's expertise is solar magic on the south mainland. They have become restless and moody in recent years and I can sense a desire to acquire more territory and power—and perhaps looking covetously at Marinea. But I'm not sure which one might have been experimenting with influencing volcanic activity as a precursor to invasion."

"Invasion! I've just become Queen and I'm immediately faced with a possible invasion?" cried Tamara.

"It's a possibility that can't be ignored, my dear," said Savea. "Place your hands in mine and let's see if our combined power can sense anything further."

"Combined power?" echoed Tamara. "What power do I have? "

"Do you mean that you don't know?" replied Savea "I know that you are aware of the shared power between Solange and me since we were once one Being. You, however, also have power that has come to you from Solange through your father. Also, I understand that you have a special crystal on your abdomen that expresses your emotions and is reflected in your hair color. All this is true?"

"Yes," answered Tamara, "except for the power flowing through my father to me. I haven't seen any evidence of it."

"Take my hands and let's see what happens."

"I'd be more comfortable if we included Solange in this experiment," said Tamara. "I'll ask Mia to send for her."

"I agree," replied Savea. "That's a very good idea."

* * * * *

The three women sat around a small table in Tamara's quarters and linked their hands. Looking upward, they watched in awe as a small transparent crystal appeared and began to grow larger. Soon it was the size of a vid screen and images were beginning to form.

"It's the Bubble Train!" cried Tamara. "But how?"

"We are seeking answers to what happened, and I think the crystal is showing us what we need to see," answered Savea. "Look!"

In the crystal, the train was moving along when suddenly it began to radiate a bright red aura with flames. "That's what I saw in my vision in the Chapel," exclaimed Solange.

The aura grew brighter and brighter until it abruptly

exploded in a flash of red light. Beneath the vaporized train, the sea floor buckled and lava spurted out. Then the crystal dimmed and faded away.

The three women sat in stunned silence. "What did we just witness?" asked Tamara.

Savea responded, "Clearly, the lava spurt was a consequence, not the cause. That train was hit by some type of destructive ray, which makes it a deliberate and premeditated act. The question now is: who was responsible?"

Tamara and Solange looked at her with puzzled expressions. "How do we find out?" asked Tamara. "Do you have any ideas, Savea?"

"Not right now. But I do want to try something. Solange, let's just the two of us clasp hands."

"What about me?" wondered Tamara.

"Just bear with me, my dear," Savea declared. "I want to try something."

Savea reached across and took Solange by the hands. A warm yellow glow surrounded them, but no crystal appeared. "That's what I thought," exclaimed Savea. "Solange and I can meld and become one, but that crystal was your doing, Tamara. It was an example of the power that you have. What's more, I've been thinking about that bright light in the Chapel that knocked us out and reunited the bond between Solange and me.

I suspect that was also your doing."

Tamara stared at Savea and her hair turned a bright violet. "Hmm," speculated Solange. "I think violet might be the expression of strong passion. Center yourself, Tamara."

"But I didn't do anything!" protested Tamara. "I just tried to help you heal in the Chapel…and I don't know how the crystal happened."

Savea and Solange exchanged glances and Savea commented, "I know you don't understand, but your power is significant—and growing. Before we go any further in trying to unravel this mystery about the train, we need to take some time to explore these powers of yours. Since the first manifestation was in the Chapel, let's return there and do some experimenting."

Chapter 8
The Power of Crystals

In the Chapel, the two Sisters and Tamara sat together and meditated. The ambient glow of the Chapel seemed to respond to their thoughts and feelings as it pulsated in an erratic rhythm. Solange turned to Tamara and touched her hand gently. "Tamara, you've been coming of age for some days now. Have you noticed any other changes in your body or appearance?"

Tamara sighed and replied, "I'm afraid so, Grandmother." She held out her hands, palms up. Each palm had an embedded crystal sparkling in the candlelight. Tamara reached up and brushed her white hair back, exposing another crystal in the center of her forehead.

"Oh my goodness!" exclaimed Solange. "When did these crystals appear?"

Savea took Tamara's hands and examined the crystals closely. "I'd say quite recently. The skin around them is quite inflamed. Do these crystals also change color like the one on your stomach?"

Tamara shook her head. "I haven't seen them change at all. Yesterday when I was crowned, they weren't there, but when I woke up this morning: there they were! I have no idea why. Do you think there is any connection to the coronation?"

Solange began to pace the floor with a concerned look on her face. "I really have no idea," she said. Turning abruptly, her flowing robe brushed a candelabra, knocking the lighted candle to the floor and igniting the hem of her robe.

"Grandmother," cried Tamara, raising her hands in assistance. Rays of light burst from the crystals in her palms and snuffed the smoldering hem before any serious damage was done. Solange stared first at her robe and then at Tamara. "How...?" she exclaimed.

Savea began to chuckle, "Well, I guess we've identified one of the powers of those new crystals. Now our challenge will be to learn how to control it—and any other emerging effects. Tamara, would you please extend your hands toward that other candelabra and try to move it?"

Tamara held her hands out in front of her and gestured toward the remaining standing candelabra. Nothing happened. She tried again. Nothing.

Savea urged, "Focus, Tamara. Remember your centering exercises and concentrate on the candelabra."

Tamara stared intently at the candelabra. Squinting her eyes, she raised her hands and white light shot from the crystals, seizing the candle stand gently and moving it slowly to the other side of the room.

"Well done!" exclaimed Savea. "So this power can be controlled. Now it is important that you practice moving things every day. Let's try one more test: Look at that candle on the floor—the one that just set Solange's robe on fire. Now try to blow it up."

"Blow it up? How can I do that?" asked Tamara.

"Direct the energy of the crystals toward and candle and mentally 'see 'the candle explode. Visualize it in your mind."

Tamara closed her eyes for a moment, then faced the candle with her palms, 'seeing' the candle vaporize—and it happened! "Wow!" she shouted. "That's amazing! So the crystals in my hands can move things, put out fires, and vaporize objects. I wonder what else they can do? And what about the crystal on my forehead? Any ideas what that one might be able to do?"

Solange admitted, "Not a clue. Not yet."

*　　*　　*　　*　　*

Later in the day, Tamara was sitting at her dressing table, staring at her reflection. I must admit, these crystals are really fascinating, she mused. A tear slipped down her cheek as her thoughts strayed to memories of her father, mother and sister. She could almost see their images in her mirror as she let her mind wander. Her thinking focused on the last time she saw them, just before they boarded the Bubble Train. But wait . . . their images really WERE in the mirror and the crystal on her forehead was glowing! It was almost like watching a projected vid! My goodness, these crystals seem to have no end of surprises! She could hardly wait to tell the Sisters of this new development!

But wait! The images in the mirror were no longer ones that she remembered. She was now watching her family in an unfamiliar place and they were tied up and gagged. What was happening? Could it be that they were still alive?

Tamara ran to the door, thrust it open and cried, "Grandmother, Savea—can you hear me?"

Solange came rushing down the hall. "Savea isn't here just now. Why did you call? Are you all right?"

Tamara hugged her grandmother and then stepped back. "I just saw my family in my mirror…and the crystal on my forehead was glowing and I think they are still alive!"

"But that's not possible," exclaimed Solange. "We all saw the Bubble Train explode!"

"I can't explain it, Grandmother. I just know what I saw," said Tamara.

"Let's go into your room and see if you can repeat this mysterious vision," suggested Solange. They walked briskly into Tamara's room and faced the dressing table. "What were you thinking before you saw the images in the mirror?"

Tamara replied, "I was remembering when I last saw them and how much I love them. And I was crying."

"Then think of them again, with as much emotion as you can."

Tamara sat quietly, gazing intently at her reflection. She remembered how excited she had been to have her whole family together and how devastating the Bubble Train incident had been. The crystal on her forehead began to glow and Tamara's image shimmered and disappeared as the faces of her family once more appeared in the mirror.

Solange gasped and cried, "It IS them…and they are alive! Can you recognize the surroundings, where they are being held?"

"No," Tamara answered. "I've never been anywhere that looks like that—all stone like a cell of some kind. And what are they wearing? It looks like some kind of fur clothes."

"Besides Alteria, our planet has two other major kingdoms, one in the north where it is quite cold and one in the very warm south. With clothes like that, I would guess that they are being held somewhere in the northern kingdom of Mosshire," replied Solange. "Savea has traveled to her home near the volcano to gather some of her belongings. As soon as she returns, we need to get together and plan what to do."

Putting her arm around Tamara's shoulders, she said, "This is a very good sign: your family appears to be alive and your powers are becoming stronger. Don't worry, my dear. We will find them and bring them home."

Chapter 9
Plotting and Planning

Two long days passed before Savea returned. The many urgent mental summonses that Solange had projected could not reach her in her dwelling near the volcano. As she entered the palace, both Solange and Tamara ran excitedly toward her. "The crystal in my forehead has projected an image in the mirror of my family being held in a cell in a cold place. Solange thinks it might be Mosshire!" cried Tamara.

"But that's impossible!" exclaimed Savea. "We saw them killed!"

"It did seem so. We certainly did see the destruction of the Bubble Train. But somehow they survived," suggested Solange. "We need to discover how and why they were captured."

"Tamara, did you see anything else in your vision that might help us determine where that cell might be located?" asked Savea.

"Besides looking like the worst kind of prison? And that they seemed to be freezing?" cried Tamara.

"Focus, Tamara. What other details can you remember? Close your eyes and replay the vision in your mind," prompted

Solange.

"I'm trying! I told you they were wearing furs."

"What kind of furs?" interrupted Savea.

"The furs were black and white...mostly black." responded Tamara. "And they were wearing hoods—black with a white border."

"That sounds like ermine...very expensive, so they are probably being treated well. That's a relief!" murmured Solange.

"But you see them in a cell, right?" asked Savea.

"I think so. I see stone block walls behind them," responded Tamara.

"Wait a minute! Could those be castle walls, rather than a cell?" cried Solange. "Do you see any tapestries or other decorations?"

Tamara took a deep, cleansing breath and was silent for a few moments. "Yes. There is a torch in a sconce on the right wall and--you are right--there is a tapestry off to the left."

Solange placed her hands on Tamara's shoulders and turned her toward the mirror. "Close your eyes, breathe, and center yourself. Concentrate on your family and then look deeply into the mirror."

Tamara obeyed, then slowly opened her eyes. Her forehead crystal began to glow softly and then with more intensity. The mirror clouded over and gradually an image appeared. Her father, mother and sister were seated on chairs near a stone fireplace. There was a fourth figure present, but the chair was turned away and she couldn't see a face. Trident looked worried and Terra appeared anxious. Trina was sobbing softly.

"They seem unharmed," commented Solange, "but definitely not pleased with their situation."

Savea asked, "Can you tell where they might be?"

"No," responded Solange. "Wait...what's that crest carved over the fireplace? Isn't that the crossed swords and ice mountain of Mosshire?"

"Of course!" exclaimed Savia. "I thought there was something familiar about that stonework. Now we know for certain that they are in the land of Mosshire, but not the reason why."

As they watched the mirror, the individual in the fourth chair stood and walked over to the fireplace. As the figure turned, the face became visible to them.

"It's Sostor, the ice magic mage of Mosshire! He's one of the Super Brothers!" cried Savea. "He must be behind this entire event. I do wish we could hear what was being said."

Tamara turned to face her grandmother. "When I was in school, I learned several languages--including the one spoken in Mosshire. I also practiced trying to tell what people were saying by studying how their lips moved. I'll try to figure out what they are saying."

Turning back to the mirror, Tamara concentrated on the lips of the four speakers. "Sostor is asking Father whether he is ready to accept his terms."

Solange asked, "I wonder what 'terms' he is suggesting."

"Father is shaking his head and refusing. Now Sostor is furious and demanding that Father abdicate the throne and surrender to Mosshire or blood will be shed!"

"My goodness," exclaimed Savea. "I told you I was worried about the Brothers' ambitions. It seems that Sostor has struck first. I wonder how he managed to spirit your family away from the train?"

"My guess," said Solange, "Is that he encased them in an ice vault that could withstand the explosion. Then it would be relatively straightforward to bring the vault to Mosshire using his ice magic."

"And he wanted my mother and sister to use as leverage to force my father to relinquish the throne," offered Tamara. "He doesn't seem to realize that we quickly arranged my coronation and that I am now the sovereign of Marinea."

"Quite right, my dear," Solange agreed. "That is why we were so intent on hurrying the ceremony along--just in case the train accident was NOT an accident."

Tamara crossed the room and sank wearily to a sofa. "Now what shall we do? We have to somehow rescue my family--but we also have to develop a plan to avoid possible war with Mosshire."

"It would be risky, but perhaps we might open a diplomatic channel to Mesarra and have a chat with Sunan, the other Super Brother. It might be too much to anticipate that he might come to our aid, but perhaps he would be willing to provide some insight into the thinking of Sostor. He's a very moody sort, possibly the result of that hot, dry climate he lives in. But he owes me a favor--I helped him build his palace several ages ago by temporarily diverting some lava into the middle of the desert," suggested Savea.

Solange agreed. "I don't think we have anything to lose. Unless, of course, he has joined forces with his brother to seize Marinea. We won't know until we contact him and even then he may be in a deceitful frame of mind."

"This all sounds very unsettling, but I'm willing to try if you think that's the best course to take," worried Tamara. "Is there any way to tell whether Sunan is being honest with us or not?"

Savea nodded. "The crystal pendant that Sunan wears is a bright orange, like the solar magic he wields. Originally it was black like Sostor's since the two of them were also one Being like Solange and me. But the development of his solar magic has had the effect of changing its color. If he is less than completely truthful, the crystal will dim in relation to the magnitude of the falsehood. If he is wearing the pendant beneath clothing, we should be extra wary as he is probably hiding something."

"Savea, would you please arrange a meeting with Sunan? Shall we use the vid screen or meet face-to-face?" asked Tamara. "I'm reluctant to leave Marinea unprotected."

"I agree," responded Savea. "Let's do the initial encounter via the vid screen. We can use as the pretext for the call that we are having a formal reception to introduce you as the official Head of State of Marinea. In fact, it might be prudent to also invite Sostor and a delegation from Alteria. It would be interesting to have all the players together so we can observe them. I'll contact him in the morning. Try to get a good sleep tonight, my dear. Tomorrow will be an important day."

Chapter 10
The Reception

Tamara turned and twisted before the mirror, trying to make sure her ensemble was absolutely perfect. Her dress was an aquamarine satin overlaid with matching lace. Small pearls were sewn randomly on the lace, enhancing the necklace of matched pearls around her neck. She wore a tiara of pearls and abalone shells on a frame of black coral. *I do look like a Queen,* she thought.

A knock at the door drew her attention. "Come in," she called. The door opened and Solange entered. "My, you look stunning!" Solange exclaimed. "Truly a Queen."

"You look elegant yourself, Grandmother. That emerald velvet gown really sets off your silver hair and eyes. And that necklace! That's the most beautiful black pearl that I've ever seen--it's gorgeous!"

"Thank you, dear. Have you been informed that all your guests have arrived?"

"Both the Brothers and a delegation from Alteria?"

"Yes. And we must keep watch on Sostor. He has come with a large contingent of 'emissaries,' but they look more like soldiers to me. Sunan has a large retinue as well, but they do look like dignitaries--somewhat plump and out of shape. I've noticed, too, that the Brothers have kept their distance from each other--and I'm not sure what that means as yet. We must never forget how powerful they each are in their own right."

Tamara looked thoughtful and asked, "How do you think we should 'play' this? Any suggestions?"

"Actually, yes," Solange replied. "I've been giving it a lot of thought and I have a plan. I think you should plan a ball in the Brothers' honor, say two months hence? And perhaps invite them to be guests of Marinea in the meanwhile. That should give Savea sufficient time, traveling through volcanic lava tubes, to reach Mosshire and look for your family."

"That's brilliant!" exclaimed Tamara. "Have you discussed the plan with Savea?"

"Oh yes," Solange confirmed. "And I believe she is readying herself for the trip even as we speak."

"How marvelous!" Tamara cried. "I do believe I am ready to confront my 'guests' now. Shall we proceed to the reception?"

Arm in arm, the two women strode to the door and into the hallway, smiling at each other as true conspirators.

* * * * *

Tamara stood at the top of a grand, crystal staircase,

surveying the glittering gathering below. Invited guests and local notables mingled together, creating a gala atmosphere. She observed the two Brothers, at opposite sides of the room.in deep conversation with representatives from Alteria. Trumpets announced her presence and she slowly began to descend the stairs, smiling graciously at the upturned faces. A rising current of applause drifted upward, dispelling her nervousness. Proceeding regally across the floor to the dais at the far end, she climbed the few stairs and turned to the crowd, nodding deliberately to each Brother. "Welcome to Marinea, honored guests. We are pleased to offer you the hospitality of our kingdom."

She turned and seated herself on the seashell encrusted throne and Solange took her seat on the blue velvet chair beside the throne. Looking up, Tamara spotted Sunan and two of his entourage approaching. Sunan presented himself with a flourishing bow, "Your Majesty. I was unaware of your coronation until I received your invitation. I congratulate you and wish you every happiness."

"Thank you, Sunan," Tamara responded. "I am pleased that you were able to join us. At the conclusion of this reception, I am hosting a small dinner party and I hope that you will be able to attend."

"My pleasure, Your Majesty," replied Sunan with a smile.

"I look forward to it." Respectfully backing away, he returned to the Mesarran delegation.

Next to approach was Sostor, the other Brother and kidnapper of her family. Tamara took a deep breath and composed herself. "Good day, Sostor. Thank you for traveling to Marinea. We are honored by your presence."

"Your Majesty," greeted Sostor with a slight bow. "I hope you and your family are well," he added.

Tamara started and then regained her composure. "Thank you for your concern," she replied icily. "I have just invited your Brother to a small dinner party following this reception. I hope you can join us."

"I would be delighted," Sostor replied. "Perhaps we can 'catch up' on family matters then." Turning abruptly he stalked away.

Tamara exchanged glances with Solange and sighed, "This is going to be a very long evening."

*   *   *   *   *

After several hours of interacting with her guests, Tamara signaled the official end of the reception. She and Solange moved slowly toward a side door that led to a small dining room. The two Brothers followed, along with representatives from Alteria, Mosshire and Marinea. Tamara seated herself at the head of the table, with Solange and Savea at the opposite end. The Brothers were directed to seats at her right and left, facing each other. Tamara thought it should be very interesting to watch the Brothers at dinner together--especially their body language.

"Sunan," she asked, "Tell me about your kingdom. Since I've never been there, I have no mental image of it."

"Think of sun...and sand. A lot of both," he replied. "My land is basically a desert, but we do have numerous sources of water throughout the kingdom, usually located in oases."

"What are oases?" Solange asked.

"Marvelous spots with palm trees and pools of water--right in the middle of the sand dunes. Oases have saved the lives of many travelers over the years. But I should continue with my description of the kingdom. We have many beautiful cities that are built around what was an oasis at the beginning. The water is so plentiful that we enjoy numerous fountains and luxuriant plantings and flowers. You must come and visit one day," Sunan offered.

"That would be wonderful. I look forward to doing so," exclaimed Tamara. "Since you are one of the Super Brothers, I imagine that your powers had much to do with the wonders of your kingdom."

Sunan looked pleased and responded, "Ineed. I must

admit that I had a hand in the creation of our magnificent land. And it is a joy to lend my skills to its continued evolution." Looking across at his brother, Sostor, he added, "I'm sure that my Brother has been equally 'influential' in the development of Mosshire."

"Yes, indeed," affirmed Sostor. "My kingdom is my greatest achievement."

"And are you both content with the current status of your holdings, or do you hope to make further improvements?" prodded Tamara.

Sunan glanced furtively at Sostor and replied, "Why do you ask, my dear? Have you been hearing rumors?"

"A whisper here and there," said Tamara. "Just enough to pique my curiosity."

"Surely you don't really take rumors seriously? Rumors are notoriously unreliable," commented Sunan. "You must have better means for gathering intelligence."

"I am open to information from a wide variety of sources," replied Tamara. "I find rumors to be tantalizing and often based in fact. To be verified, of course," she added.

"And just how do you 'verify' " asked Sunan.

"Different ways," she replied, "and undoubtedly similar to your methods of verification."

"Intriguing," commented Sunan. "What would you deem

your most reliable source?"

"I'm afraid that's a state secret," answered Tamara. "I should return the question."

"As you say, my dear. Some sources of intelligence simply cannot be shared without compromising internal security," Sunan responded.

Tamara shrugged and turned to Sostor. "Do you want to add to this conversation, my Lord?"

Sostor glanced at his Brother and then faced Tamara, peering at her intensely. "It would be of great interest to me to learn how each of you manage your efforts at spying."

"Surely you cannot expect us to reveal such sensitive information, Brother?"

"You already have," grinned Sostor. "I noted that you did not deny that such efforts exist!"

"Of course not," Sunan laughed. "Intelligence gathering is a ruler's secret weapon and we would all be defenseless without it. What is important is the effectiveness of such an operation, both in securing and then using the information. But enough of such senseless chatter. How are things in Mosshire, Brother?"

"Quite well, thank you," Sostor responded. "Our economy is growing and our people appear to be content."

"Content? Not happy with their lives?" Tamara asked.

"Rulers bear the responsibility of securing the people's physical welfare," commented Sostor. "Happiness is not a requirement."

"My, my," Sunan chided. "Surely you wish your people to have happy lives, do you not?"

"And are your people filled with joy and happiness, Sunan? I rather doubt it, living in that excessively hot location," probed Sostor.

"On the contrary," Sunan laughed. "My people wake each morning wreathed in smiles and look forward to enjoying the day. I not only see to their physical needs but their spiritual ones as well."

"Are their good spirits related to living in warm climes and not having to expend time and energy keeping warm?" asked Tamara.

"Possibly, to some degree," Sunan answered. "But I prefer to believe that my regime fosters an atmosphere of caring and enjoyment. We all try to help each other when there is need-- and everyone loves a good party!"

"Such nonsense!" exclaimed Sostor. "Our subjects are content to live within a structure of rules and obligations. They feel secure in such an environment."

"Security is a two-edged sword, Brother. Too much 'Security' can lead to discontent and rebellion."

"Rebellion!" laughed Sostor. "There is little chance of that. My domestic forces are well-trained and supremely loyal to me."

"Are you so certain?" asked Sunan. "History shows that rulers often delude themselves."

Tamara watched this brotherly exchange with interest. Knowing that Sostor had her family in custody lent a macabre tone to Sostor's comments. She asked Sostor, "Just what would you do if some of your citizens were displeased with their living conditions and decided to express their disapproval?"

Sostor's face darkened and he stood suddenly, pushing himself away from the table. "I refuse to respond to these absurd questions." He strode angrily from the room, followed quickly by his retainers. A heavy silence hung in the air.

"Well, that was a dramatic exit!" commented Sunan. "My dear Queen Tamara, please accept my apology for my Brother's poor manners."

"No apology is required from you, Sunan," Tamara assured him. "Please continue to enjoy your dinner."

Conversation in the room resumed as the servers brought in tray after tray of new delectables. With a sigh and expressing fatigue from the long day of festivities, Tamara rose and wished everyone a good night's sleep. Sunan kissed her hand and bid her goodnight. He explained that he and his Brother would be departing early in the morning. She thanked him for coming, wished him safe travel and, with Solange, left the room.

Once in her private quarters, she collapsed on a blue divan and asked Solange for her impression of the evening.

Solange took a seat next to Tamara and replied, "Watching the Brothers interact was enlightening. They appear to be polar opposites in many ways and seem to personify the lands that they rule. Sunan comes from a warm land and is certainly personable in his demeanor. Sostor, on the other hand, is as cold as the land he governs."

"What an interesting assessment." Tamara pondered as she stood and began to pace back and forth. "You and Savea are also different in your natures, but not so dramatically. And while Savea, like Sunan, is also drawn to a warm environment and does have a fiery temper, you are certainly not cold and unapproachable as Sostor seems to be."

"Thank you for that," laughed Solange. "My guess would be that there was some interference when the four of us were thrust into existence in order to supplant and thereby dilute the power of the two Super Children."

"But what kind of interference? And to what end?" asked Tamara as she crossed the room and stood before the mirror.

She carefully removed her crown and placed it on a side

table. As she did so, her white hair was swept to the side, revealing the crystal in her forehead--which was pulsating with orange light. "Oh my," she cried, turning to face her aunt. "Now what is happening to me?"

Solange ran to Tamara and gathered her into her arms. "I'm not sure," she soothed. "Come and sit down for a minute and we'll try to figure it out."

Sitting side by side and with hands clasped, they looked into each other's eyes. Peering intently, Solange asked, "Has this ever happened before? What color is that crystal normally--and is it the same or different than the others?"

"Before you taught me to control my emotions, my hair and my tummy crystal would change color—together--to reflect what I was feeling. Now that I am in charge, both remain white and no one can know my thoughts or moods. The new crystals on my forehead and palms have followed suit— until just now." replied Tamara.

"Then I would say that your crystal is sending you a warning," advised Solange, "And I would not be surprised if one or both of your uncles are involved. I'm sending for Savea. We need as many minds--and powers—as possible to sort this out. We'll meet her in the Chapel. It's the most neutral and protected area that we have. Come, my dear. We must hurry."

Chapter 11
Decoding a Puzzle

The Chapel was suffused in a dim golden light as Tamara and Solange entered. Soft music played in the background as they walked up the aisle to the front. A moment later, Savea came rushing in, her black locks tousled and a red robe loosely tied around her.

"I received your urgent summons. What has happened?"

Tamara hugged Savea and walked to a nearby cushion. She straightened her gown—there hadn't been time to change into more comfortable clothing. Brushing her white hair aside to uncover her forehead, she pointed to the exposed crystal, which still glowed orange, although not as brightly as before. "I used to be able to control the color of both my crystals and my hair. Now the crystal in my forehead seems to have a mind of its own," she exclaimed.

Savea peered intently at the crystal and then touched it gently. "Oh my!" She cried. "It's very warm. Does the crystal on your stomach also radiate heat?"

"No, not at all," answered Tamara. "What do you think is happening?"

"Well, in color theory, blue is a cool color and orange is

warm. I'm guessing that you felt a strong kinship with your Uncle Sunan. He comes from a very warm climate," suggested Savea. "Do you agree, Solange?"

Solange thought a moment and then added, "Well, I know that I find him much more appealing than his Brother. But why such a strong response? I believe that more is going on here. Tamara, close your eyes and think about your Uncle Sunan. Tell me about your thoughts and feelings."

Tamara closed her eyes and sat quietly. "I feel pleasantly warm and quite calm," she answered.

"Now think about your Uncle Sostor," prodded Solange.

Tamara gasped and blurted out, "Fire! I see fire and hear people screaming! I'm not sure where I am. Yes, I do! It's the Bubble Train and it's been hit by a fiery ray!"

She shivered and pulled her robe more closely around her. Looking into a nearby mirror, she gasped, "The crystal on my forehead has turned blue! Is that because I started to think about Uncle Sostor?"

Solange nodded and suggested, "Can you try and focus on your parents and Trina? Think about some good memories that you shared."

Tamara reached for the pew behind her and carefully sat down. Her crystal began to glow a soft pink, throbbing gently.

"I remember how happy I was when I first met Father and

then when Mother and Trina awakened. It was so amazing to have my whole family around me."

Savea took Tamara's hand and asked, "Can you remember a bad dream that you might have had?" Tamara thought a moment and then looked into Savea's eyes, remembering...

"I'm afraid. Dark night. No moon. Rustling leaves. I'm afraid. Hearing footsteps in the distance. Getting closer. Coming up behind me. I'm afraid. I'm afraid. Footsteps louder. Looking behind me. Seeing nothing. Hear an owl. Footsteps faster. Getting closer. I'm afraid."

Savea put her arms around Tamara and murmured, "And your crystal turned black as night. Your forehead crystal has become a mirror reflecting your emotions. I think we have two alternatives: Learn to better control those emotions--or style your hair to cover your forehead!"

Solange chuckled and commented, "Well, the hairdo would be easiest...but I think stronger self-control should be our goal."

"Fine," agreed Tamara. "But how do I go about it?"

Solange thought for a moment and then suggested, "Let's repeat that routine that you just tried with Savea. But as soon as you bring up the original image, immediately think of its opposite. We'll see if there is any effect."

"All right. The first thing I thought of was Uncle Sunan

and my crystal glowed orange."

"And it's beginning to do so now. Quickly, think of your Uncle Sostor."

Tamara wrinkled her nose and tried to focus. The orange faded and blue began to emerge.

Savea cried, "Think of Sunan.then Sostor.then Sunan. Keep your thoughts shifting back and forth."

Tamara closed her eyes while her aunts watched her crystal closely. The blue glow faded and orange began to emerge. The two colors bounced back and forth in concert with her thoughts until a steady white glow appeared and stayed.

Savea cried, "Perfect! Now all you need to do is practice opposing thoughts until you regain control."

Tamara sighed and hugged Savea. "That sounds like a real challenge. I'll do it and let's hope it works!"

"Since the three of us are together," mentioned Solange, "What did you think of tonight's dinner--and the abrupt departure of Sostor? He certainly has a dramatic streak!"

Savea replied, "Like most autocrats, I'd guess a bit of insecurity. He may impose those rigid living conditions as a counterpoint to potential uprisings rather than as a sincere philosophical belief system. Which leads me to another question: Why do you suppose he engineered the abduction of your parents and sister? What could he hope to gain from such actions?"

Looking worried, Tamara brushed her hand across her forehead, exposing the crystal—which had turned a brilliant shade of red! She swayed in her chair and slid forward to the floor.

"Tamara!" cried Solange. "What is it? Please open your eyes."

Savea helped Tamara back into her chair as Solange rang for assistance. Tamara's eyes fluttered and her head rested on Savea's shoulder. There was a soft knock at the door as an attendant entered with a pitcher of water, followed by a strikingly attractive woman with green eyes and matching hair. "I'm Dr. Astarte, the new court physician. Is the Queen ill?"

Savea answered, "We don't know. She just collapsed."

Dr. Astarte performed a brief examination and commented, "It appears that she just fainted. I have some smelling salts in my bag." Waving the vial beneath Tamara's nose, she watched carefully for signs of returning consciousness. However, Tamara's eyes remained closed, her body limp.

"She has a red crystal on her forehead," commented Dr. Astarte. "How long has that been there?"

Solange responded, "Apparently, she has had crystals on her body all her life. She also has crystals on her stomach and palms. They seem to change color in tune with her emotions. My sister, Savea, and I have been working with her to control them."

Dr. Astarte nodded, "I'm glad you are helping her. I had heard tales of the Queen's crystals, but I didn't know if they were based on fact. I've never known anyone who actually had crystals. Do you know how the Queen acquired them?"

Solange replied, "Our cosmology tells us that when the two Super Children were reduced in power as their essences were split by the Parent Super Beings and their crystal orbs divided into two, the crystal shards that were released were swept up by a whirlwind and lost in the mists of history. I suspect that there is a connection between those shards and Tamara's crystals."

"Has the crystal on Tamara's forehead always been red?" asked Dr. Astarte.

"No," answered Solange. "Originally, they were all clear. But with the onset of puberty, they began to change to reflect her feelings."

"Has red ever appeared before?" asked Dr. Astarte.

"No," replied Savea. "But she has been entertaining her two uncles. One of them, Sostor, is believed to have kidnapped her family after causing a fiery crash of the Bubble Train! Perhaps she has sensed some danger, and that has produced the red color."

"Perhaps. Does anyone know anything about her family and where they might be located?"

"We believe that they are being held in the North...in the kingdom ruled by Sostor. But we don't know why they were kidnapped."

Dr. Astarte frowned and thought for a minute. "Is there any way that we could find out their whereabouts for certain? The 'why' of the kidnapping may take some time to determine."

"Without the knowledge gained from Tamara's visions and the colors of her crystals," reminded Solange, "I don't know of any other sources of intelligence."

"Remember the new initiative that Tamara began to create diplomatic presences in other kingdoms?" Savea asked. "Were embassies established in Mosshire and Messara?"

"I believe so," replied Solange. "Dr. Astarte, have you heard any news about embassies in other lands?"

"Actually, I have," she replied. "One of my close friends has relocated to Mosshire with her family. She is the new Ambassador there. However, I don't know how helpful she can be. Apparently, Sostor is quite the autocrat and all communications are monitored. Embassy officials are only welcome by invitation."

"But enough talk of politics. I think we should help the

Queen to her room now so she can rest."

* * * * *

Tamara stretched slowly and opened her eyes. Looking around her bedroom, she found herself alone. Swinging her legs over the side of her bed, she carefully stood and tested her strength. Feeling comfortable, she walked toward her dressing table and sat down. She raised her eyes to her mirror and brushed her hair aside. Staring intently at the crystal on her forehead, she was relieved to see that the red had reverted to its original white tone, matching her basic hair color.

"I wonder what happened to me. My forehead crystal had never turned red before." she thought.

A soft knock at the door interrupted her musing. She turned toward the door and asked, "Who's there?"

"It's Dr. Astarte. May I come in?"

Tamara walked slowly to the door and opened it. "And who are you? I don't believe we've met. "

"Technically, we met yesterday. I'm the new Court Physician and I was called in to treat you when you fainted in the Chapel."

"Thank you for your ministrations. I don't know why I fainted. It's not something I ever do."

Dr. Astarte smiled and asked, "Do you mind if I take your

vitals?"

Tamara turned and walked to her bed. Sitting gingerly, she placed her hands on her lap. Dr. Astarte quickly checked her over and sat on a chair beside the bed. "What do you remember just before you fainted?"

"I was thinking about my family, worried about their safety. I was looking in a mirror and brushed my hair aside, exposing the crystal on my forehead. I was shocked that it was no longer its normal white color but had changed to bright red. That's all I remember until I woke up here in my bedroom."

"That sounds like you fainted from the shock of seeing your changed crystal," commented Dr. Astarte. "Do you have any idea why your crystal changed color?"

Tamara closed her eyes and tears slipped down her cheeks. "I was practicing alternate thinking about the two super brothers in order to control the color of my crystals. As I was checking on the results in the mirror, I remember that I had a vision of fire when I was focusing on Sostor. I felt the heat of the fire and a strong sense of anger emanating from him. The feeling was abnormally strong compared to previous times I had focused on him. That's when my crystal's color suddenly became bright red. It also became very hot, like the fire."

"I have no experience with crystals," claimed Dr. Astarte, "But my observations and instincts tell me that your crystals hold real power and that they are active, not just passive reflections of your emotions."

"Really?" exclaimed Tamara. "So are you suggesting that, in addition to trying to neutralize the colors through these exercises, I should be exploring how to enhance and control the colors themselves?"

"Exactly," replied Dr. Astarte. "I have a question for you. I've been told that the two Super Sisters have a history of not getting along. Do you know why?"

"Apparently they were both in love with my grandfather—and he chose Solange. Savea became both hurt and enraged. Her response was to take herself to the volcano and vent her feelings through earthquakes and lava flows. It has been only recently that they are acting like sisters again."

Dr. Astarte stood, walked over to the mirror and faced Tamara. "What happened to cause this reconciliation?"

"I'm not sure." Tamara replied. "We were all together in the Chapel and they were arguing. I reached out to them and held their hands. Suddenly, there was a bright light and they both fell to the floor in a faint. When Savea awoke, her demeanor had softened."

"I see. Do you have any explanation for what occurred?" asked the Doctor.

Tamara shook her head and said, "I don't. I've wondered

about it often."

"Let me offer a possible interpretation." said the Doctor. Walking across the room, she sat next to Tamara on the bed. "Consider this: What if it was your power, through your touch, that realigned the relationship between the two sisters?"

Tamara frowned and asked, "But how did that happen? What 'powers' could I possibly have?"

"That question requires more insight than I can offer. Let's invite the two Sisters to help us figure it out. I'll see if they are available and be back in a few minutes." Dr. Astarte exited the room and Tamara walked to the mirror to check on her forehead crystal.

*   *   *   *   *

"May we enter?" asked Solange.

"Of course," replied Tamara. "Is Dr. Astarte with you?"

"Yes, along with Savea. Dr. Astarte shared her theory about your power being channeled through your touch when we were in the chapel. How did you feel when that happened?" asked Solange.

"I was so focused on trying to stop the bad feelings between you two that I grabbed your hands...and then you both fell to the floor. I don't recall any particular feelings other than that."

Solange took Tamara's hand and asked, "Would you allow me to probe your mind after inducing a relaxation and meditative state? It might allow some memories to surface."

"Of course. I trust you. What do you want me to do?"

"Come over to your bed and lie down." Solange sat on a chair next to the bed and held Tamara's hand. Savea pulled a chair to the other side of the bed and held Tamara's other hand. The two Sisters closed their eyes and began chanting softly. Tamara lay still, listening to their soothing voices. Her eyelids flickered and slowly closed. Even the lighting in the room seemed to respond and decrease to a faint glow. A silvery mist began to swirl near the ceiling and gradually lowered to envelop Tamara's body. The crystal on her forehead began to pulse in a slow rhythm, changing from white to a matching silver. As the pace of the rhythm increased, Tamara's body began to lift from the bed and gently float upward.

When the Sisters noticed that Tamara's hands had risen, they opened their eyes and stopped chanting. "She's floating in the air," cried Savea. "How is that possible?"

"She is still within a trance and is not awake," answered Solange. "I would agree that she is definitely powerful. The crucial question is: How do we help her to recognize and control her innate powers so that they do not control her?"

Savea grasped Solange's hands and asked, "What do you

remember about the incident in the Chapel? The one where we both lost consciousness and fell to the floor after Tamara touched us."

"I remember her entering the Chapel, rushing towards us as we yelled at each other, and putting her hands on ours. Then darkness."

Savea nodded in agreement, saying "That's what I remember as well. So neither of us actually saw her power in action but certainly felt it as we sank to the floor."

"So how should we proceed? Oh my goodness, look at Tamara! The crystal on her forehead that had turned silver is sending out beams of silver light toward her wrists!"

"Incredible! Those beams seem to be encircling her wrists and pulsing rapidly. But look closely...the beams seem to be solidifying into silver bracelets!"

Solange stood and peered closely at the silver crystal in Tamara's forehead. "The silver hue of the crystal is fading and the crystal is returning to its normal white color. And Tamara's body seems to be sinking back to the bed. How extraordinary."

Tamara stirred and slowly opened her eyes. "What has happened? Did I faint? What are these silver bracelets on my wrists...where did they come from?"

"The silver in your forehead crystal streamed toward your wrists and created the bracelets. Your crystal is now back to normal. While all this was going on, you levitated off the bed and were floating in the air. How do you feel now and how do the bracelets feel on your wrists?" asked Solange.

"I'm not sure. I'm tired, which is foolish since I haven't done anything this morning."

"Except float in the air!" exclaimed Savea.

"How did I do that? And why?"

"That's one of the mysteries that we need to solve," replied Solange. "Now, what about those bracelets? Do you have any idea why they are there?"

"No," responded Tamara. "And I don't seem to be able to remove them."

Savea picked up a small statue from a table and tossed it to Tamara, "Here, catch!"

Tamara instinctively raised her left arm so that her bracelet could block the toss and the statue sailed across the room.

"I suspected that defense might be one of the purposes of the bracelet, and I am right!" boasted Savea. "I also believe that there is an offensive potential and we need to investigate that possibility." commented Savea. "Solange, I think you and I need to pursue these ideas and then work with Tamara to develop whatever powers she possesses, both known and unknown."

"Tamara, you've had a remarkable day and you need to

restore your strength. Please take this day to rest and reflect. We will meet with you tomorrow to plan strategy," said Solange.

The two Sisters exited the room with Dr. Astarte, leaving Tamara to ponder what had transpired that day. She decided to take a relaxing soak in the tub in the hope that she would be able to sleep well that night. As the warm water swirled around her, she began to doze. The bracelets on her wrists began to glow, increasing in intensity as she deepened into a sleep state and slowly slid beneath the surface of the water. Suddenly her arms reached toward the ceiling and her body rose into the air, floating across the room and gently sinking onto her bed. Still asleep, she snuggled into the covers and the glow on her bracelets subsided.

Chapter 12
The Puzzle Deepens

The next morning, Tamara stretched in bed and sat up. She noticed that her bed was wet and called for Mia. As Mia entered the room, Tamara beckoned her over to the bed. "Mia, I just awakened to find myself lying in a wet bed. Do you have any idea why my bed should be wet?"

Mia picked up some of the wet bedding and held it to her face. "It smells like the scent of your bath salts, Your Majesty. Did you take a bath last night before retiring?"

"I did. But I have no memory of coming to bed. Isn't that strange?"

Mia nodded. "Perhaps I should call Solange and Savea?"

"That's probably a good idea. And please bring new—and dry—bedding when you return."

Mia left and Tamara was alone. She walked to her closet and selected a dress and underclothes for the day. As she was changing into the dry clothing, there was a knock at the door. "Enter," she called.

Solange and Savea entered and walked toward Tamara. "Mia told us that you had a strange night involving a bath and a wet bed. Do you have any idea what happened?" asked

Solange.

"No, I don't. The last thing I remember is sitting in my tub, letting the warm water swirl around me so I could relax before heading to bed. My eyelids were heavy and I was feeling wonderful. When I woke up I was in a wet bed with no idea how I got there," answered Tamara.

"Your father recently had security cameras installed around the palace. Do you know if any were placed here in your bedroom?" asked Solange.

"What do the cameras look like? I haven't noticed any in here," responded Tamara.

Savea and Solange looked at each other and shrugged. Savea said, "We know they are small and inconspicuous, but we really haven't paid any attention to them. Let me call Security and ask." She walked over to a seashell intercom mounted on a nearby wall.

"Someone will be right up to explain the security system," said Savea. "In the meantime, shall we have breakfast delivered?"

"That's a really good idea," said Tamara. "I'm starving!"

*   *   *   *   *

Breakfast dishes were being cleared away when there was a knock at the door. "Enter," prompted Tamara.

A staff member in the uniform of Security came in and bowed to the Queen. "I'm from Security. My name is Brise. You have questions for me, Your Majesty?"

"Yes. When my father, the King, had security cameras installed, were any placed in my quarters?"

"Yes, Your Majesty. The King was always concerned about safety, while also being cognizant of privacy issues. Therefore, the cameras were designed to be unobtrusive and worked into designs that did not make them obvious."

"I have not been aware of any cameras here in my bedroom. Can you point them out to me?" asked Tamara.

"Of course. Look at the line of seashells joining the walls to the ceiling. They are decorated with pieces of coral. Except that on one on each wall there is a tiny camera instead of a coral piece. Can you pick it out?"

Tamara gasped, "I never would have guessed! Now I have to look closely." She walked slowly around the room studying the seashells.

"I still can't tell. Those cameras must be really small."

Brise agreed, "Indeed they are. It's a truly ingenious system. Look at the second seashell from the far corner. The faux coral is pale pink. Can you see it?"

"I can. And that's a camera?"

"It is. There's a camera lens behind the pink cover."

"I'm very impressed, Brise." said Solange. "I'm assuming that the surveillance is being recorded. How long is the recording saved?"

"For two weeks."

"So you have a recording of yesterday and last night?" Savea added. "Can you bring it here for us to view?"

"Of course," said Brise. Walking to the door, he promised, "I'll get it and be back soon."

*   *   *   *   *

Solange walked over to the door and admitted Brise who was carrying a strange looking machine. "This is our replay unit for the security system," said Brise. "I'll put it on this table and we can take a look at last night."

Tamara and the Sisters pulled chairs over so they could look at the screen. Brise turned on the replay unit and the screen filled with images of Tamara's bedroom. The watchers saw Tamara sitting in her bathtub and heard soft background music playing. A sequence of images showed Tamara starting to dose. As she succumbed to sleep, she slipped beneath the surface of the water. Suddenly her arms reached for the ceiling, her bracelets glowing and pulsing. Still sleeping, she rose into the air and floated over to the bed, gently descending and curling up in the covers.

The watchers gasped and looked at each other in amazement. Solange cried, "Those bracelets saved your life, Tamara! Clearly, the bracelets have powers that are protective of you."

Tamara stood and started pacing. "What can this mean? I'm so confused. Why didn't my gills activate? Somehow the bracelets are connected to my crystals, but I don't know how or why!"

Savea offered, "We know there is a connection. The bracelets were created by the crystal on your forehead, remember? And if your crystals are indeed some of the shards released when the Super Children and their crystals were subdivided, then there may be a force at work that we know nothing about."

"As for your second question: You were in a bath that was not salt water. Apparently, the bracelets could tell the difference," proposed Solange.

"And why me? Why am I the only person who has crystals on the body? I'm not related to the Super Beings as far as I know," commented Tamara.

"That's not true," interjected Solange. "Saves and I are two of the four divisions from the Super Beings. And I am your grandmother. Therefore, you do share some of my bloodline."

"And Solange and I support the theory that your crystals

are connected to the shards released during the division," added Savea. "It is possible that the Creator Being has set these events into motion."

"But why?" asked Tamara. "And another point: If I'm of your bloodline, obviously my father is also. Could that be why he was kidnapped by Sostor? Could it be a political power play? And why doesn't he have any crystals or other signs of magic? And then there's my sister, who hasn't exhibited any signs either."

"Those are very good questions," replied Solange. "Clearly, your bracelets are protecting you. That is a very positive thing. We will continue to monitor any additional activity involving those bracelets. But the issue of bloodline is more complex and we will need to conduct some tests on you before proceeding. Are you willing to comply?"

"Yes, of course," answered Tamara. "I think that's an avenue we should pursue immediately, especially since it may shed light on the motives for my family's kidnapping. My questions seem to be answered by more questions!!!"

"I'll call Dr. Astarte and ask her to arrange the necessary tests," proposed Savea. "Let's meet back here as soon as the tests are completed."

*   *   *   *   *

It was late in the day when the test results were back. The Sisters and Tamara had returned to her bedroom to discuss the findings. Dr. Astarte was waiting for them. She invited them to sit together on a couch near the door. "Your blood tests showed a special marker that is not found in the blood of other citizens of this kingdom or in the blood of your mother. However, your sister does have that marker. Curiously, your father does not," reported Dr. Astarte.

"I have a theory about that," said Solange. "Please test my blood and that of Savea."

"Actually, I have your results on file," added Dr. Astarte. "And your guess is correct. You two have the same marker."

"But my son, the King, does not?" asked Solange.

"That's correct," replied the doctor. "My explanation would be gender. You are descended from the female Super Being and your son is male. I believe the marker follows the female genetic line. And your sister has not yet reached puberty, so we don't know how she will be affected."

"I know that she doesn't have any crystals on her body like I did," said Tamara.

"But the marker can manifest itself in other ways and we will just have to monitor her—once we get her back home," said Dr. Astarte.

"Meanwhile, since my powers are originating from you,

Grandmother, can you help me identify and control them?" asked Tamara.

"I'll do my best to help you," agreed Solange, "But I don't have any experience with crystals. This will be an adventure for both of us. Savea, do you have any suggestions for us?"

"Obviously I don't trust Sostor, but I'd like to consult Sunan. Let's invite him back and we can put our three Super Children brains to work," advised Savea.

"That's a really interesting idea," said Tamara. "He may also be willing to share his thoughts about the kidnapping. I'll contact him immediately."

Chapter 13
Sharing Ideas and Strategies

Tamara looked pensively at her wrists and the bracelets encircling them. There hadn't been any change since the incident yesterday in her bedroom. Today is the day that Sunan would arrive and her excitement was growing. She had dressed in a favorite blue gown for the occasion and put finishing touches on her hair. Walking toward the door, she checked out her appearance in the mirror. All the crystals on her body were staying white so far this morning. She hoped that would continue through the day.

Leaving her bedroom, she glanced to the right. A staff member in blue livery was rushing down the corridor. "Your Majesty, the Bubble Train with Sunan aboard has arrived."

"Please bring him to the Chapel and I will meet him there. Also ask the Sisters to be present."

"At once, Your Majesty."

* * * * *

Tamara entered the Chapel and took a seat near the front. Her gaze wandered around the room, taking in the soft lighting and the stained glass renderings of sea-related images. She looked down at her wrists, noting that the bracelets remained silver and no pulsing was present.

Hearing the Chapel door open, she stood and turned around to greet Sunan and the Sisters. "Thank you for accepting my invitation. We have much to discuss," said Tamara.

Sunan embraced Tamara and commented, "I was really intrigued by your invitation—especially since my brother Sostor was not included."

"Can you guess why?" asked Tamara.

"Guess is the appropriate word," said Sunan. "I do not have firsthand knowledge, but I have heard rumors that your family has been kidnapped and that Sostor had something to do with it."

"The rumors are correct," confirmed Tamara. "My family was en route on the Bubble Train to the mainland when the kidnapping occurred. I have had visions of them in captivity and it is a very cold environment. My conclusion is that Sostor is the perpetrator."

"But why? What would be his reason for such a grievous attack?" pressed Sunan. "What did he have to gain?"

Taking his arm and leading him to the front of the Chapel, Tamara explained, "This attack is one of the reasons for asking you here. We need to join our knowledge and intuitions and see if we can figure it out."

"One of the reasons. What are the others?" he asked.

"Other questions are concerning crystals," Tamara replied. "What do you know of the cosmology and history of life on this planet?"

"I'm familiar with the cosmology resulting in the Great Division that split the two Super Children into four: two male and two female. Sostor and I are the males and Savea and Solange are the females. We all wear pendants containing crystals like this," he added, pulling out his pendant with a gold encased crystal from under his shirt. The two Sisters also displayed their pendants, one crystal encased in gold and the other in silver.

Tamara looked at the pendants with awe. "I'm really impressed," she said. "Does it make a difference if the crystal in the pendant is surrounded by gold or silver?"

Sunan responded, "I've often wondered about that, but I don't know."

Tamara then proceeded to show Sunan the crystals on her body and asked, "Do any of your crystals ever change color?" Sunan shook his head. "Mine never has." Savea and Solange also responded negatively. "Why do you ask?" inquired Sunan. "I was born with just one crystal in the center of my abdomen. It remained white like my hair until I reached puberty. Then it began to change color as a reflection of my emotions. I have worked diligently with the Sisters to control and neutralize the crystal's color—an effort which is even more important now that a crystal has appeared on my forehead and elsewhere. In fact," she said, holding up her arms, "My forehead crystal shot rays toward my wrists and created these bracelets which are also color-capable and generators of power."

Solange added, "Apparently the emergence of crystals on Tamara's body are related to the sudden presence of a small whirlwind like the one in the cosmology saga that scooped up the crystal shards released when the Great Division occurred. Savea and I have a theory that Tamara's crystals are some of those shards. If we are correct, and we believe we are, the existence and power of the crystals makes sense. After all, Tamara is my granddaughter and therefore is of the Super Being lineage."

"My goodness," cried Sunan. "That's an awareness that had never occurred to me! But has the King, her father, exhibited any crystals?"

"No," answered Solange "and we believe that is because the lineage runs through the female progeny because Savea and I are of the female line."

"So Sostor and I would represent the male line and any male descendants may inherit powers if not crystals?"

"We believe so," affirmed Solange. "Do either of you have any offspring?"

"I don't know about Sostor. I, regretfully, have never produced any heirs."

"Would you like to adjourn to the Private Dining Room for some lunch?" asked Tamara. "I'm really famished."

Everyone agreed and they left the Chapel to take a dining break.

* * * * *

Once they had enjoyed a delicious lunch, they decided to remain in the Private Dining Room to continue their discussion of issues and strategies.

"From what I've learned so far today," Sunan commented, "There are actually two distinct areas that we need to explore: 1) My brother, Sostor, and his motives, and 2) Tamara and her crystals. Which one would you like to focus on first?"

"They are both important," said Tamara. "But my family's welfare is foremost in my mind. You don't seem to know much about Sostor and his ambitions. Am I correct?"

"Sadly, you are. There has been deeply held sibling rivalry ever since we came into existence. I've tried to extend a hand of friendship, but he has consistently turned me away. However, I've been worried about his behavior and have authorized covert incursions into his kingdom."

Solange started pacing back and forth. "Have you discovered any intelligence about what Sostor is up to?"

"Very little, I'm afraid. But there are a few nuggets that we might explore. As I mentioned earlier, Sostor and I have never shared information or worked together on any projects. We've been very separate in how we develop and govern our respective kingdoms. We do have trade treaties in place that were negotiated by our ambassadors and, as of now, there are no sanctions in effect although there have been in the past."

Solange stopped her pacing. "Please forgive me but walking about helps me think. You just said that you have ambassadors. So why do you need covert intelligence?"

"Because our ambassadors are confined to our embassy grounds and are only allowed to leave when Sostor wants to see them. He is almost paranoid about potential spies and is very secretive. Conversely, his ambassadors are allowed total access in my kingdom. I have nothing to hide."

"So what have your intelligence agents discovered?" asked Savea.

"They have reported that the palace is under extraordinary security and no reason has been given. Further, borders have been closed and no one may enter excerpt by invitation. Just before I left to come here, I was informed that present trade missions have been suspended without notice. Sostor seems to have cut all ties to the outside world. I met with his ambassadors and they are as baffled as I am—or so they seem."

"Now what could be his endgame, I wonder," pondered Solange. "If he is seeking to expand his power, what would he gain by isolating himself?"

"A weapon!" exclaimed Tamara. "He's developing a new weapon and he's forcing my father to help him by threatening the rest of my family!"

"What expertise does your father have in terms of weapon development?" asked Sunan.

"He knows nothing about weapons but he knows how and where my kingdom may be vulnerable to attack! The real question is why Sostor would want that information!"

Sunan shrugged and sighed, "Solange, you mentioned expansion of power. I probably know Sostor better than anyone even though we are not close. Think about what might be useful in that regard."

Solange gasped! "Oh no! It's not the kingdom...it's the crystal pendants!!!"

"Exactly," Sunan agreed. "I have a hypothesis. The four Super Children each have a crystal pendant as a result of the Great Division. If Sostor can mount a successful invasion of this kingdom and, in the process, manage to take you Sisters captive, he would have control of three of the four pendants. And I'm not even talking about Tamara's crystals. That would leave one pendent—mine—to ward off the power of three plus crystals. I consider such a scenario extremely threatening to my interests."

Now everyone was pacing back and forth. Tamara walked over to Sunan and gave him a hug. "I am so sorry. When I invited you here, I had not even considered what Sostor's endgame might be. What are you going to do now?"

"I know we need to talk about your problems with crystals, but I really think that I need to return home to increase my defenses. When I have done all I can, I promise to return and we will pick up on this discussion."

"I understand," said Tamara. "Be safe and keep in touch."

Sunan bowed and left the Chapel.

Chapter 14
Preparing Defenses

After Sunan's departure, Tamara wiped her eyes and looked somberly at the Sisters. "What shall we do now? How can we protect this kingdom? And we still haven't figured out what the crystals and bracelets mean."

Savea looked at Solange and took her hands. "If we join the powers of our crystal pendants we can create a defensive barrier around the kingdom so that Sostor and his weapons cannot penetrate."

Solange agreed, "That would be a good first—and temporary—step. But we also need to focus on how to get my son and his family back."

"Once we figure out how my powers work, and Sunan returns, we can combine our crystals and move on Sostor. But I'm also worried that Sostor may have designs on the two of you and I'm concerned for your safety."

"We can't wait for Sunan's return," said Solange. "The amount of time he may need to maximize his defenses is uncertain. I think we are on our own."

"I agree," added Savea. "Solange and I will create the defensive dome barrier and then I will summon lava to reinforce it. Can either of you think of any vulnerability that we should address?"

"It is likely that any weapons Sostor might develop would be related to cold temperatures and ice," commented Solange. "I think your suggestion about lava should take care of any frozen technologies."

"It's possible that a weapon could be airborne. Would those defensive measures stop an attack from above?" asked Tamara.

Solange took out her crystal pendant and affirmed, "The barrier we are going to create with our pendants will create a dome that can protect against airborne. But the lava will work primarily at the base of the dome so we need to think of something to stop frozen airborne missiles."

Walking to the Chapel door, Tamara ordered, "Please use your powers to create the defensive dome and then meet me in my quarters for afternoon tea and a continuation of this discussion."

* * * * *

When the Sisters joined Tamara for tea, she began the discussion by focusing on potential vulnerabilities in the kingdom. "One entry point that needs to be addressed immediately is the Bubble Train itself. The airlock between the ocean and the palace station needs to be seriously reinforced. Can the joint power application that you used to create the defensive dome be adapted to protect the airlock as well?"

"Definitely," replied Solange. "But, in addition, we need to create a special security password to be used when the train needs to move through the airlock."

"We also need to create and train a defensive security force that will be a first strike unit when an attack is detected," added Tamara. "Oh, I just had another thought. What if Sostor creates some kind of ray to somehow freeze the ocean around us in spite of its salt content? That could suffocate us. How can we defend against that?"

Savea poured a refill of tea and suggested, "My control of the undersea volcanoes is extensive. I will look into how the lava can be weaponized in the event of an attack. There is no doubt that any polar assault could be neutralized."

"That's comforting," sighed Tamara. "I don't feel as helpless as I did earlier today. One more thing that just occurred to me: If my family was kidnapped so that pressure could be applied to my father, Sostor is seriously underestimating him. I believe that my father is an intelligent and creative King with an innate cleverness that Sostor may not be aware of."

"I definitely agree," affirmed Solange. "My son is a

worthy adversary for any dictator such as Sostor. He is an honest and capable King, but also a crafty and clever politician. It will be interesting to see how this plays out."

"So what are our next steps?" asked Tamara. "My sense is that we should consider three initiatives. First, Savea should immediately begin to study how her unique relationship with the volcanoes can be utilized in a defensive capacity. Second, Grandmother can conduct an investigation of our vulnerabilities and what the King might do or say to Sostor when pressed. And finally, I will increase my efforts to understand and expand my emerging powers. In that regard, I will appreciate any assistance that the two of you can offer."

Looking at Savea, Solange said, "I think we can both agree with this strategy. Shall we meet again in the Chapel tomorrow morning after breakfast and share our progress?"

Tamara led the way out of her quarters and all went their separate ways.

*　　*　　*　　*　　*

The next day, Tamara and the Sisters reconvened in the Chapel. Savea spoke first, "I've been experimenting with the volcanoes and their lava output. Those volcanoes are very active and the output is significant. In order to take advantage of this resource, I would recommend digging a channel surrounding the kingdom and directing the lava into that channel. Further, I do have sufficient power to vaporize some of the lava to create a defensive dome over the kingdom that would deter any attack and yet allow the ocean to surround us. That would be challenging, but I believe it is doable."

"Is that really possible?" asked Tamara. "How would such a dome be held in place and yet allow the ocean to circulate?"

"The laws of physics would not apply. The process would be constructed and managed through the strength of my powers—which are considerable," explained Savea. "I think that my plan would produce an adequate defensive strategy for the kingdom. Solange, have you made any progress on identifying other vulnerabilities?"

"I've been trying to think like my son, but it is difficult. I wish he were safe and home so that we could make meaningful identifications. But, failing that, I have a couple of ideas. First, there is the Bubble Train. It is an essential transportation link with the mainland, but it is also a link that can be breached. I propose that we safeguard the train by running it under the ocean floor rather than on top of it."

"How could that be done? And how quickly?" asked Tamara.

"I, too, have powers that could be useful here," responded Solange. "I would create an underground tunnel using volcanic heat energy that would do two things at once: melt the solidified lava that lies beneath the ocean and immediately reapply it to create new tunnel walls for the train to use.

"A second vulnerability is, of course, the captive status of my son and his family. I am hoping that we can partner with Sunan to rescue them as soon as possible. I will be contacting him as soon as this meeting has ended. Once Sostor is neutralized, we can focus on returning things to normal."

"And that leaves me," said Tamara. "I've been practicing with my crystals and trying to decipher what they can and cannot do. One thing that I discovered is that the crystals seem to activate and enable my new bracelets. And these bracelets are definitely defensive as we suspected. But they can also focus crystal power as an offensive weapon. I've been able to target and destroy items at will."

"That's amazing!" cried both Sisters.

"Yes," agreed Tamara. "I think our three-pronged approach to protecting this kingdom will be effective. Let's get to it!"

Crystal Saga
Genesis Explored

D. E. Weingand

Prologue

I'm Queen Tamara and I'm the ruler of the undersea kingdom of Marinea on the planet of Akura. I became ruler suddenly because my father, mother and younger sister, Trina were kidnapped from the Bubble Train they were taking to the mainland kingdom of Alteria. My kingdom needed an interim ruler and I was next in the line of succession.

I was born with a crystal on my stomach. When I reached the age of puberty, my body added crystals to the palms of my hands and also one to my forehead. No one could understand why the crystals appeared or why they suddenly began to change colors reflecting my emotions.

Our cosmology tells us that in the beginning of Time, the Creator sought to have company and made two Super Beings, one male and one female. Each was endowed with a crystal pendant, the source of their power.

Subsequently, the Super Beings created two offspring, male and female, each with personal crystal pendants that were originally part of the ones worn by their parents. However, fearing that just two children would have too much power, the Super Beings/Parents decided to split each Super Child and their pendants into two, resulting in two male and two female.

The two females, Solange and Savea, reside in my undersea kingdom of Marinea. Savea lives close to several volcanos. Solange has a special role: she is my grandmother!

The two males have two separate kingdoms: Sostor in the cold north and Sunan in the warm south. Each Super Sister and Brother wears a crystal of power in a pendant around the neck. When all of this took place, some crystal shards remained and a tornado whisked them away. No one knows why or where they were taken.

We held a reception when I became Queen and invited both Sunan and Sostor, as well as friends and dignitaries. It was interesting to watch the Brothers interact. They seem to be polar opposites. So far, I have not been able to determine if either of them has hostile intentions toward my kingdom or the Sisters, who are my partners in trying to understand my crystals and identifying my related powers.

We have also been busy designing strategies to defend my kingdom and rescue my family. We have developed a three-pronged strategy, but, so far, it is on paper only.

It seems my life is full of challenges: both political and personal. All of these challenges seem to have connections to the cosmology that the Creator put into motion. I'm so glad that the Sisters are my allies. If they were not, I would feel so alone.

Chapter 1
Dreamscape

Tamara lay quietly on her bed. She had been in a dreamless sleep when, suddenly, she began to stir. The crystal on her stomach was beginning to pulsate and change from one rainbow color to another. As Tamara became more agitated, the crystal started to project images onto the ceiling. The images were encased in individual bubbles that seemed to portray a sequence of events:

- *A single Creator Being*

- *The Creator Being took some creative essence and formed two complementary Super Beings joined by a silver cord: one male and one female. The male wore a black crystal pendant and controlled the night, moons and stars. The female wore a white crystal pendant and controlled the day and its twin golden suns.*

- *The Super Beings lived in a crystal castle atop a tall mountain that was accessed by a crystal staircase.*

- *A room in the center of the castle housed a huge crystal orb of power that controlled all of creation*

- *and captured light from the twin suns, showering creation with rainbows.*

- *The male and female Super Beings created a single male and female offspring of themselves, each having a personal crystal orb of power.*

- *To prevent these two children from having and possibly abusing too much power, the two parental Super Beings split the essence of each child into two, resulting in two original and two mirror beings—a total of four Super Children.*

- *As a result of this transformation, the power orbs given to each child cracked in half, leaving crystal shards behind. The large crystals were encased in pendants of special metals: gold for the two original children and silver for the two mirror beings.*

- *A whirlwind appeared and whisked the remaining shards away.*

Tamara cried out and sat up in bed. She gazed at the ceiling where the images still remained. Trembling, she ran to the door and called for Solange. She heard footsteps running down the hall and was relieved when Solange appeared.

"What is the matter?" exclaimed Solange. "Are you all right?" Solange entered the room and hurried to Tamara's bed.

Tamara threw her arms around Solange and started to cry. "I had a disturbing dream that frightened me. Come and look at my ceiling!"

Solange stared with fascination at the ceiling.

"My goodness," she said. "You were dreaming about the creation of our world. How did you learn about it?"

"My mother told me the story when I was a child," explained Tamara. "I was young and didn't fully understand it."

Solange raised her arms and directed a beam of silver light toward the ceiling. "I want to preserve these images and we can discuss the meaning later. However, your dream woke you up and you still need to get more sleep. Let me tuck you back into bed."

Solange soothed Tamara and made her comfortable. She glanced at the ceiling and saw that the images were fading. Wishing Tamara a good rest, she exited the room.

Tamara settled into her soft covers and fell into another dreamless sleep.

* * * * *

The sky was brightening when Tamara started to squirm and whimper again. Bubbles containing images once again appeared on the ceiling. In addition, her crystal was sending rays of rainbow light around the room. Unlike the previous images that had depicted the creation of the Super Beings, this new series showed how their actions shaped the world.

- *All land on the planet Akura formed one large continent.*

- *The four Super Children had authority over land and sea.*

- *As siblings, they began to argue and fight.*

- *The Super Being Parents decided to punish them and hurled an asteroid at the planet.*

- *The four Super Children used their pendants to force power at the asteroid and managed to deflect it.*

- *The Super Children were so relieved that they shed many tears which fell to the ground and became beings with no powers.*

- *These various peoples multiplied and learned to live in harmony, viewing the Super Children as deities worthy of worship.*

- *The Super Being Parents became jealous of this piety and caused the Great Quakes which broke the single continent into three pieces.*

- *After another massive tremor, one of the three pieces sank beneath the sea, leaving only a small island behind which became Alteria.*

- *The Super Being Parents allocated the two remaining pieces of land to each of the sons; the two daughters were assigned to the sea.*

- *The Super Children were told that they would be left alone to care for the planet for many millennia as part of their education.*

- *The crystal castle would be hidden from their eyes until some future time when they would all be reunited.*

As the bubble images shimmered on the ceiling, Tamara rolled from side to side, tears streaming down her face.

Suddenly, the door to her bedroom opened and Solange swiftly entered. She walked quickly to Tamara's side and placed her hand on Tamara's forehead. Tamara quieted and softly reentered a dream state. Solange brought a chair to her bedside and directed a silver beam once again to the ceiling to capture the images. As she settled in to keep watch, the bubbles on the ceiling faded away.

Tamara shivered and called out for her mother. Solange took her hand and stroked it softly. "Rest, my dear. You are only dreaming." As Tamara resumed her even breathing, more bubbles began to appear on the ceiling. Images of settlements and diverse populations emerged in the bubbles.

- ***The first bubble showed many small pieces of land connected by bridges. Some were forested, but most were covered by ice. The people had fair skin, blonde hair and very blue eyes.***

- ***The second bubble depicted a great desert and the people had hair, eyes and skin that was dark in tone.***

- ***In the final bubble a great sea was populated by underwater residents with silver hair and eyes. Retractable gills enabled them to breathe beneath the water. There was also a small island in the midst of the sea.***

Solange once again directed a beam of light at the ceiling to capture the images. When she had finished, she gently put her hand on Tamara's shoulder and said, "It's time to wake up, my dear. We have much to discuss."

Chapter 2
Interpretation Begins

Tamara stretched and slowly opened her eyes. Sitting up in bed, she turned to Solange and yawned. "Is it morning?" she asked. "I've been having such unusual dreams that seem both interesting and unnerving."

Solange replied, "Yes, it is morning and your dreams have been more than interesting. You seem to have an unconscious grasp of your heritage that appears to be quite comprehensive. Do you remember any of these dreams?"

"Just impressions. No details. Why would I be having such disturbing dreams?"

Solange held her hand and replied," When I entered your room the second time, you were clearly having a vivid dream that was upsetting you. Your crystal was sending rainbow rays around the room and I had the impression that your crystal was trying to alert you to something. What is the first thing that you can remember from the dreams?"

Tamara gazed at her crystal, which was softly glowing, and responded, "I have so much on my mind: my family's kidnapping, the two Super Brothers and their possible intentions, and other matters of state. I think my crystal is telling me that I need to revisit my heritage and try to start at the beginning in order to understand the present. But I wish Mother were here to guide me."

"That would be nice," said Solange. "But don't worry. I know as much—or possibly more—about your roots as your Mother did. We can figure this out. Right now, why don't you get dressed and come down to breakfast. I'm going to make some copies of the bubbles with their images that I took from the ceiling. Then we'll begin to try to make sense of them."

* * * * *

Tamara picked at her soft boiled eggs as she tried to remember her first dream. She frowned at the effort as she slowly raised her fork. The savory flavors melted in her mouth but she barely noticed their goodness. Frustration took her attention and she sighed audibly. *"Why can't I remember?"* she thought to herself. Pushing her plate away, she stood and started pacing the floor. As she walked back and forth, she noticed that Solange had entered the room.

Solange crossed over to the table and sat down next to Tamara's chair. "Why don't you take your seat and finish your breakfast?" she asked Tamara. "It's getting cold."

"I'm just so confused," Tamara complained. "I know my breakfast was well prepared but I could barely taste a thing.

"All I seem to be able to do is to try unsuccessfully to remember my dreams. How can we attack this puzzle if I have nothing to contribute?"

"I may be able to help with that," Solange suggested. "Please place your hands upon your crystal and close your eyes."

Tamara sat down, pulled her skirt down a bit and covered her crystal with her hands. She felt a warmth flow upward, surrounding her entire body. She tried to open her eyes but could not. "What is happening to me?" she asked.

"I've put you into a relaxed state that I hope will release some of the barriers that your mind has erected to block your memory. I'm not sure where those barriers came from, but I suspect that a spell is involved," Solange replied.

"A spell! Who could have done that to me—and when?" exclaimed Tamara.

"I have a theory," responded Solange. "Have you felt differently since entertaining the Super Brothers?"

"Now that you mention it," said Tamara, "I have been more tired and sometimes I struggle to put words together in a meaningful way."

"I thought so," Solange agreed. "I have noticed those efforts and wondered about them. Leave one hand on your crystal and reach out with the other to me."

Tamara blindly reached toward Solange with her right hand. As she grasped Solange's fingers, she felt a cooling breeze waft over her from head to toe. Her eyes flew open and she could suddenly see clearly. "What did you do to me?" she asked, "My head feels incredible and all the fuzziness is gone!"

Solange explained, "I cast a reversal spell to combat whatever magic was affecting you. I don't know which Brother spelled you, but until we find out, please don't trust either of them."

"I'll be careful. However, the only one who would benefit from affecting my memory is Sostor. We know that he engineered the kidnapping of my family."

"You may be correct," agreed Solange, "But we need actual evidence to be certain. Now, how is your memory? Can you recreate any of the dreams?"

"Let me think a minute. I'd like to try to access them in order if I can. I am sure that I have access to the Creation story, so let's talk about that first," suggested Tamara.

"That's a good idea," replied Solange. "What is the first thing you remember?"

"There was an original Creator Being that wished to have someone with whom to share the splendor and decided to create two Super Beings: one male and one female. They were joined by a silver cord so that they could join their power. The male's power was housed in a black crystal that controlled the night and its attributes; the female had a crystal that was white and had power over the day and its suns. Do I have that right?"

Solange nodded her head and affirmed, "Exactly right. What is the next thing you remember?"

"I saw the two created Super Beings living in a crystal castle atop a tall mountain that was accessed by a crystal staircase. Then I saw a room in the middle of the castle where a huge crystal of power was located. I'm guessing that it somehow controlled all of creation. The twin suns seemed to send light that animated the big crystal. There were rainbows everywhere. That's all I saw in that vision," added Tamara.

"You're doing very well," assured Solange. "That is how the Creation story was communicated to us. But there is some additional information. Can you recall anything else?"

Tamara closed her eyes and breathed deeply. "Yes!" she exclaimed. "Like the Creator earlier, the two Super Beings tired of being alone. They seemed to want to make offspring. I saw them focus a combined stream of power from their crystals toward the huge crystal and two Super Children emerged: male and female. Is that correct?"

Solange smiled and commented, "Yes, you have most of it right, but there is a slightly different interpretation. Originally, there was only a single Super Child replica of each of them that they endowed with crystal orbs of power. But then they worried that these creations might have two much power and they split each replica and crystal orb into two. Now there were four total Super Children, each having more limited power with their crystals encased in precious metals designed to be worn as pendants: gold for the two original children and silver for the two mirror beings."

"I did find the vision confusing. Thank you for clarifying it," said Tamara. "But there is one more thing. I seemed to see little crystals moving in lots of different directions. What was that all about?"

Solange explained, "Legend tells us that a great whirlwind arose and swept up those crystal shards. No one knows what happened to them after that. It is still a mystery."

"Wow! That's quite a story," commented Tamara. "But I still feel that there is more to talk about."

"There is," agreed Solange. "You have remembered one-third of the dreams. Meditate on what we've discussed and we will consider the other portions tomorrow."

"Thank you for helping me, Solange," Tamara added. "That was a huge piece of the puzzle. I think meditation will help me organize my thoughts."

Solange hugged Tamara and quietly left the room.

Chapter 3
Continuation

Solange knocked softly on Tamara's door the next morning. Hearing no response, she gently turned the doorknob and entered the room. Walking to Tamara's bed, she softly called Tamara's name. Tamara stirred and opened her eyes.

"Is it morning already?" she asked. "My sleep was very restful, but I feel like a few more hours would be wonderful."

"I understand," empathized Solange. "But we really need to continue our discussion of your dreams. Shall we share our thoughts over breakfast?"

"That sounds like a good idea," agreed Tamara. "I'll meet you in about thirty minutes, if that works for you."

"That's fine," Solange replied. "I printed out some copies of the images from your dreams. We can begin our conversation with those images as a starting point."

* * * * *

Tamara entered the Private Dining Room and joined Solange at a large table. Stacks of paper showing familiar images were already on the table. After taking a seat next to Solange, Tamara glanced at the images and expressed amazement at how accurately they depicted what she remembered from her dreams.

"I'm really impressed with the images," commented Tamara. "How did you capture them and reproduce them so clearly?"

"One of my powers allows me to do this," explained Solange. "I focus a stream of energy at the desired objects and then I can transfer their images to another medium."

A server appeared to take their breakfast orders, so the discussion had to be suspended until the meal had ended. As soon as the breakfast dishes were cleared, the discussion resumed.

"I have so many questions," said Tamara. "For example, in the first dream, the Creation story was fairly straightforward. But there was no explanation of where the crystals came from or how the power was activated."

"Creation was initiated by the Creator Being. All power flowed from that Creation. No one knows how this transpired. All we do know occurred after that initial Creation. The connection between crystals and power, while mysterious, does follow a certain logical progression," explained Solange.

"And that progression seems to be deeply affected by emotions such as anger, loneliness, greed, and jealousy," added Tamara.

"Yes, those traits are definitely present and color the way the story unfolds," agreed Solange. "That's an astute observation and we must remember to keep it in mind as we try to unravel the meaning of your dreams."

"Another question: Why am I the only one with a crystal on her body? I'm not aware of any other person who has one," asked Tamara.

"I don't know," responded Solange. "It certainly does make you unique and special. I think we must also keep that question front and center as we consider your dreams."

"And what do you know about my family? Has any genealogy been done? I know my mother and father and sister, of course. I've heard of my grandfather, but I never met him and I was told that he was the reason that my father had to return to Marinea, leaving the family behind. I also know that you are my father's mother and my grandmother. Beyond that, I have no information."

Solange rose and walked across the room. Turning to face Tamara, she replied, "Savea and I once had a good relationship. We lived under the sea and used our powers to help the Marineans prosper. Then, one day, this handsome man entered our lives and we both fell in love with him. We learned that he was the heir to the throne of Marinea and was required to select a bride. He wooed each of us and we became obsessed with him and became rivals for his affection. Ultimately, he chose me over Savea and the bond between Savea and me fractured. Once I gave birth to your father, your grandfather became ill and his health gradually became fragile. He lived for many years in a weakened condition; just before he died, your father, who had gone to live on land, was called to return to the sea."

Tamara asked, "Who was king before my grandfather?"

"I don't know," answered Solange. "Savea and I never paid attention to politics until your grandfather entered our lives. I'm not aware that any genealogical research has ever been done."

"Don't you think that is odd?" queried Tamara. "I would think that royal families would be carefully chronicled."

"Now that you bring it up, it is strange. I'm not aware of any history of the Marinean royal family. When I think about it, I wonder if any magic was involved. That's another puzzle that we need to keep in mind," added Solange. "It seems that your questions are important and a search for answers is definitely indicated. I'm beginning to think that Savea and I have been under a spell and any curiosity we might have had was taken away from us, leaving only jealousy and hostility behind. If I'm correct, she and I have to get to the bottom of this mystery. With your permission, I'd like to invite her to join us in this discussion."

"Of course," agreed Tamara. "Let's meet here in the Private Dining Room for afternoon tea. I'll send her an invitation right away."

Chapter 4
Joining Forces

The Private Dining Room was empty when Solange and Tamara entered. They selected a table and ordered tea and cookies for three. A few minutes later, Savea swept into the room.

"Your invitation sounded urgent," she commented. "Has something happened?"

"Indeed," answered Solange. "Tamara has been having strange dreams that result in images encased in bubbles appearing on the ceiling of her bedroom. We have been trying to understand the meaning of these dreams and images and, in the process, Tamara has been asking some very important questions to which I have no answers. We are hoping you can help us with this mystery."

"I'll certainly try," Savea promised. "What are some of the questions?"

Tamara asked, "Who was king before my grandfather? And related to that is the issue of genealogy. Has any been done? I can't find anything."

Savea looked confused. "You know, I never thought about that before. I wonder why that is."

Solange jumped to her feet. "I knew it!" she exclaimed. "Savea, when Tamara asked those questions, I felt confused as well. Then I suspected that you and I had been placed under a spell! We must get to the bottom of this!"

Tamara joined hands with Solange and Savea. "I think there is some connection to the unpleasantness between the two of you as well. I'm aware that both of you were smitten by love for my grandfather. But I believe that the conflict that arose between you was too strong a response. Can you think back to when you worked together to improve life under the sea?"

Solange and Savea both exclaimed, "Yes!"

"And then I felt so depressed and angry, as if my world had fallen apart," cried Savea.

"So did I," Solange agreed. "It was as if a cloud of sadness surrounded me and I could not think clearly."

"That's a perfect description of a spell," said Savea. "Now how can we get rid of it?"

"Join hands with me, Savea. We are powerful Beings, two of the four Super Children. Surely we can work together to break this spell," pleaded Solange.

Holding hands, the two Sisters walked to the middle of the room and began to softly chant. A golden mist began to surround them. In the middle of the mist, lightning streaks churned and the Sisters disappeared into the center of a tornado. Tamara was blown across the room and she clung to a nearby pillar. The wind was so strong that her clothes shredded, exposing the crystal on her stomach. Rainbow rays surged from the crystal and entered the tornado that encased the Sisters. Suddenly there was a loud explosive sound and the tornado disappeared, leaving the Sisters unconscious on the floor.

Tamara ran across the room to where the Sisters lay. She placed her hands on their foreheads and felt her own warmth pass into their bodies. Tamara called for help and two attendants entered with weapons drawn. Not seeing any observable enemies, they carefully picked up the Sisters and placed them on couches arranged against the nearby wall.

"Please call for a doctor," ordered Tamara.

The attendants swiftly left and in a relatively few minutes, a doctor appeared. "Dr. _____? I'm sorry, I don't recognize you. Are you new to Marinea?" asked Tamara.

"Yes, I am," answered the doctor. "I arrived recently. My name is Dr. Angelus. I am a medical doctor, but I also have a degree in magical science. From what I understand, I think the latter may be of most use."

"What exactly do you understand?" Tamara pressed.

"I've learned in my short time here that these two ladies are the Super Children that have made so many contributions to Maninea. And that you, My Lady, are the ruler of this kingdom. Apparently, all three of you have many powers and are quite remarkable Beings. I am honored to serve you. What has happened here?"

"My grandmother and her sister were trying to break a suspected spell involving both of them. As they were chanting, they were engulfed by a gold mist, and then there were lightning streaks, and a tornado. Rainbow rays from my stomach's crystal surged toward them and there was an explosion. The tornado disappeared and I found them unconscious on the floor."

"That's a very succinct and helpful description, Your Majesty. I'd like to examine my patients now," said the doctor.

As Dr. Angelus began to assist them, the Sisters began to try to sit up. "Easy," said the doctor. "I need to tend to your injuries. Please move as little as possible." Both Sisters complied and the doctor's examination went swiftly.

Tamara was surprised at some of the tools the doctor had at his disposal. Some looked familiar, but others seemed to employ amazing technologies. While the doctor was assessing their potential injuries, Solange and Savea looked at each other and smiled. Turning their attention to Tamara, they reported that their attempt to break the spell had not been going well. However, when the rainbow rays from Tamara reached them, the spell broke into small fragments which the tornado swept away.

"What can you now remember," asked Tamara.

"It was definitely a spell," Solange answered. "I don't know who cast it, but it was extremely powerful. I'm able to remember how Savea and I behaved prior to the spell and also how strangely we acted afterward. I'm so happy all of that is now in the past."

"I agree," commented Savea, "But the effects of our discord must now be addressed. And we need to investigate the intent of the spell. What did the spell caster hope to accomplish?"

"Let me ask again," Tamara urged. "Who was king before my grandfather?"

Both Sisters looked at each other and replied, "No one."

"What?!" exclaimed Tamara. "You mean my grandfather was just installed as king by an unknown someone? For what purpose? And Solange was "chosen" to marry him? Again, for what purpose?"

"I don't think it mattered which one of us married him," suggested Savea. "I believe the intent was to manipulate this kingdom and create a division between Solange and me."

"That makes sense," agreed Solange. "We have a deeper mystery than we anticipated."

Dr. Angelus interrupted their conversation and commented, "I don't believe you will have any lingering physical effects, but please contact me if any memory or psychological issues arise and I will return immediately." Bowing, he exited the room.

Tamara sank into a nearby chair. "This has been quite a day," she sighed. "Grandmother, what was it like to be married to this mysterious grandfather? Savea, what about grandfather was so appealing to you?"

Solange replied, "My answer now will be quite different than what I might have said if you had asked me yesterday. Once we were married, he seemed to lose interest in me. We had physical relations about once a month when he seemed to know that I was fertile. After your father was born, your grandfather almost withered before my eyes. I became a virtual single parent as your grandfather did not participate in helping to raise your father. Looking back, it was strange and I certainly did not understand his disinterest in us. He became a recluse and I rarely saw him. In his absence, Savea and I actually ran the kingdom."

Savea added, "Your grandfather was a very handsome man. Almost too handsome to be real. I was totally captivated by him and felt crushed when he chose Solange as his bride. I became enraged and you know how badly I behaved. He ignored me completely after their wedding and I was devastated. I'm ashamed to admit that I took my anger out on Solange rather than on him. Please forgive me, Solange."

Solange said, "You were under a spell, Savea, as was I. There is nothing to forgive. I think it might be useful to create scenarios about possible perpetrators and motivations. Since at this point, we don't have any evidence, we can use our imaginations and see if anything feels right."

Tamara suggested, "Let's pretend that we are creating a game. One input would be our new knowledge of the past. Another would be the kidnapping of my family. A third would be the tension between the Super Brothers. Finally, there is the mystery of my crystals."

Savea nodded her head. "That would give us a framework for brainstorming. I think it would be a good place to start.

Chapter 5
Of Magic and Magicians

Savea, Solange and Tamara gathered around the table that still held tea and cookies for three. As they savored the mid-afternoon treat, Tamara broke the silence, "I suggest that we initially consider a structure based on time. If you agree, we should begin with the issue of genealogy. So far, our knowledge of my family's history begins and ends with grandfather. Who was he? Where did he come from? Was he a real person? Or a synthetic Being produced by person or persons unknown? And, if the latter, to what purpose? Are there any other possibilities?"

Solange sipped her tea and mused, "Now that the spell is broken, I still cannot recollect anything prior to being introduced to your grandfather. There must have been some type of government, but I don't know what it was. Savea, do you remember anything?"

"I don't recall being so intimately connected to volcanoes before being rejected by your grandfather. The volcanic activity is tied in my mind to the emotions of hurt and anger," answered Savea.

Tamara stood abruptly and cried, "That's it! There were

two spells: One was based in logic and memory and the other affected emotions. We broke the first spell, but not the second."

"But I still can't remember," complained Solange.

"Perhaps your emotional ties to grandfather are still covering up the memories," offered Tamara. "I'm going to send for Dr. Angelus again. His studies in magical sciences may provide some insight."

* * * * *

There was a soft knock at the door and Dr. Angelus entered.

"Thank you for coming so swiftly," said Tamara. "We are seeking information about spells that you may have learned in your magical studies. Could Solange and Savea have been affected by two different types of spells: one directed to memory and one centered on emotions?"

"Most certainly," answered Dr. Angelus. "Are you suggesting that only one type of spell was broken?"

"Yes," responded Tamara. "And even though I believe that the memory spell was eliminated, I think Solange's memory is still clouded by the spell on her emotions."

"That would be a very powerful and clever incantation," affirmed Dr. Angelus. "I have never encountered such a spell, but that doesn't mean it doesn't exist."

"How would you suggest we proceed to eliminate an emotion-centered spell? Do you know of any counter spells that we could try?" asked Tamara.

"Solange, would you allow me to use magical hypnoscanning to enter your brain? It's an advanced form of hypnosis that can focus on multiple areas of the brain," proposed Dr. Angelus.

"Yes, of course," responded Solange. "We need to explore every possibility to solve these questions."

Dr. Angelus led Solange over to a nearby couch and had her lie down comfortably. "Close your eyes and try to relax," he urged. "There will be no pain. But it is important to keep your eyes closed so they will not be endangered."

As Solange complied, a silvery mist proceeded from the doctor's hands and surrounded her body. An image of her brain appeared just above her and the doctor pointed out the areas that housed memory and emotions. The memory area was surrounded by a purple cloud emanating from the emotion area.

"You were right, Your Majesty," exclaimed Dr. Angelus. "Her emotion area has dominated the memory area. Do you have an alchemist on your staff?"

"I do. She is quite talented. Shall I send for her?" asked Tamara.

"Definitely. Before I collaborate with her, I want her to see the result of this scan," replied the doctor.

* * * * *

Several hours later, Dr. Angelus reentered the room with a beaker filled with a purple liquid. "I'm sorry you had to wait so long. The alchemist and I have created a potion that I believe will clear the confusion from Solange's brain. And I recommend that Savea also partake of this potion."

"We used the time to continue our deliberations and then take a much-needed rest. Thank you for including me, doctor," said Savea. "I am also undoubtedly affected by that second spell."

The doctor walked to the table and filled two teacups with the purple potion. He gave one to Savea and then moved toward Solange, who was still lying on the couch. He waved his hand and the silvery mist disappeared. Taking Solange's hand, he helped her sit up. Giving the other cup to her, he asked both of them to drink. The two Sisters drained their cups and Savea sat down near Solange. Dr. Angelus helped them both to lie down and again asked that their eyes close. After sending the silvery mist again toward the two women, images of their brains rose into the air. No longer did a purple cloud surround the memory area of Solange's brain and Savea's scan looked completely clear.

"I believe that the problem is now resolved," claimed Dr. Angelus. "Let's see what they remember now." He waved his hand and the mist evaporated. Helping them sit up, he asked them how they felt.

Solange and Savea looked at each other and began to cry. At the time of the Great Quakes and the sinking of land beneath the sea that created Marinea, we became advisors to a king," said Solange. "It was a turbulent time and I don't recall any family members there with him."

"Nor do I," affirmed Savea. "In fact, I remember little about the king. You and I managed the kingdom for him. He was away for long stretches of time. Then, suddenly, he returned with an adult son with whom we both fell in love." Turning to Tamara, she continued, "This is looking more and more suspicious to me. What do you think?"

"I agree. But one more thing. This question may seem strange, but Solange, what do you remember about Savea's appearance when your joint self was separated into two Super Children?" asked Tamara.

Solange replied, "Our original Super Child had white hair and blue eyes. When we became two separate entities, we arrived under the sea and our hair and eyes turned silver like the other residents of Marinea."

"But that's not what Savea looked like when I first met her," commented Tamara. "She had dark hair and eyes—and still does."

"It was when your grandfather chose me as his bride," recalled Solange, "that her appearance and personality changed. She left immediately to live in the volcano and all communication between us ceased."

"I vaguely remember," said Savea. "It feels like a bad dream. I recognize the truth in what you say, but it doesn't feel real to me. Did something happen to change our relationship back to one of love and sisterhood?"

"I think it was something I did," admitted Tamara. "When we first met, you were vengeful and angry. You were about to return to the volcano and a cloud formed around you. I grabbed your hand and pulled you out of the cloud. Then I also reached for Solange's hand and there was a great white light. After that I remember nothing.

"When I came to, I could tell that time had passed because the candles on the Chapel altar had almost burned out. Both of you were still unconscious on the floor. When the two of you awoke, the relationship between you had mended."

Solange and Savea looked at each other and smiled. Then they turned to Tamara and hugged her. As the three of them embraced, a golden glow surrounded them. When they separated, Tamara gasped, "Savea, your appearance is different again!"

Savea ran to a nearby mirror and exclaimed, "My hair and eyes have changed color! Now my hair is reddish gold and my eyes are amber with flecks of red! But if a change occurred, why didn't my looks return to the original silver color?"

Solange gazed at her sister and suggested, "Perhaps it's the effect of living in the volcano for so long. I like it. It's very attractive."

"But why do you think it shifted from the original silver to black in the first place?" asked Savea.

Tamara responded, "Your black hair and eyes could have been part of a spell. And one more thought: We are family. I have white hair that reacts and changes color in response to my emotions. Perhaps your black hair and eyes were a reaction to the intense anger and hurt you were feeling at being summarily rejected by grandfather."

"I never thought of that," cried Savea. "Our genetic makeup could certainly play a role in the changing color of my hair."

"And presumably mine," added Solange. "But my hair didn't change color. It stayed silver."

"Grandmother, your personality is calm and peaceful. You don't let emotions control your thinking. But Savea is volatile and temperamental. It makes sense that her hair would reflect what she was feeling," suggested Tamara.

Solange responded, "I think the mystery goes much deeper. What I'm about to say may sound like a fairytale, but please bear with me. You know that we live in a world of mythology and magic."

"Of course," agreed Savea and Tamara.

"Well, what if the original king that we remember wasn't real? What if he was part of an elaborate spell? He could have been an android or a hologram—or another magic-wielder in disguise," said Solange.

"Wow!" cried Tamara. "Is that even possible?"

"Actually, it is very possible," answered Solange. "And then, think about how he would leave for long stretches of time, and suddenly he returns with a full-grown son who somehow proves so attractive that both Savea and I fall in love. While the king was away, no one ever knows where he went. That is an open question."

"This doesn't sound like a fairytale at all," asserted Savea. "Let me add another thread to this evolving tale. The full-grown son who became your husband and eventually Tamara's "grandfather"—was he even real? Solange, you said right after your wedding, he became ill and was often out of sight because of his alleged poor health. The only actual fact we know from that time was the birth of your father, Tamara, and we could hypothesize a number of scenarios for that."

Tamara added, "We could, indeed. Plus I think that both of you must have been put under a spell that made you believe this tale, fall in love, and have that cause a serious break in your relationship to keep you distracted."

"My goodness," exclaimed Solange. "The plot thickens and becomes more and more plausible. If the three of us can agree that we should continue unravelling these mysteries, then we need to create a list of questions to serve as a starting point."

"It's getting late," said Tamara. "Let's reconvene tomorrow at breakfast and bring independently created questions to discuss. And let's not forget our plans for a three-pronged approach to protect the kingdom: a safer underground route for the Bubble Train; the rescuing of my family from Sostor; and understanding the powers available to me through my crystals and bracelets. We need to get to work on those."

"I'll see both of you in the morning," said Savea. "Try and remember any dreams you may have. They may contain useful clues."

"That's a good point," agreed Solange. "We'll need all the clues at our disposal to prove or disprove our hypotheses."

Chapter 6
The Breakfast Meeting

The three women gathered over a sumptuous breakfast of crab cakes, pancakes and berries. After satisfying their hunger, they began to discuss the events of the prior day and their growing suspicions.

Tamara offered to begin. "I feel confident that we are not indulging in idle speculation. The exact nature of the king and his son will emerge, I believe, as we unravel the motivation and the person or persons responsible for this conspiracy."

"That seems sensible to me," agreed Solange. "Let's consider who might benefit from such an elaborate deception—and why."

"My first thought is that only two people—besides ourselves—could have sufficient power to create such an ongoing illusion. The Super Brothers. Since we are victims in this scenario, the Brothers should be the focus of our initial analysis," proposed Savea.

"Let's consider each Brother's physical appearances as a first clue. Sostor has blonde hair, fair skin and very blue eyes. Sunan has dark hair and eyes, plus very tanned skin from living in such a sunny climate," offered Tamara.

"I'm not sure that's relevant," commented Solange. "Both the king and his son physically resembled the residents of Marinea."

"But wouldn't that be important to the design of the ruse?" answered Tamara.

"I definitely think so," responded Savea. What else do we think was unusual about them?"

Solange added, "Their behavior. Both were only in our sight for short periods of time. Then they were absent without telling anyone."

"Perhaps they just assumed they didn't have to," proposed Tamara. "Some men, especially powerful ones, just behave that way."

"But, as I said before, Savea and I were responsible for jointly managing the kingdom when they were away. I always wondered why they left without any notice," complained Solange.

"I think that's definitely peculiar," added Savea. "And when they returned, it was always suddenly and without warning."

"Almost as if magic were involved," Tamara joined in. "Did they ever act as if they were confused or puzzled when they came back?"

"Not at all," answered Solange. "They behaved as if they

had never been gone."

"Then I propose that we agree that such inappropriate behavior might indicate that they were magically produced and not real beings," said Tamara. "Where do you think they went when they disappeared?"

"If they weren't real beings, perhaps they were stuffed in a closet?" joked Savea.

"That's actually a possibility," admitted Solange. "But to what purpose?"

"So they wouldn't be discovered," said Tamara. "If they had stayed in plain sight for long periods of time, someone might have figured out that they were artificial."

"Solange, you were married to Tamara's grandfather. Did you ever suspect anything about his identity?" asked Savea.

"It never crossed my mind," answered Solange. "But now that I think about it, when he came to my bed on our wedding night, it was at night in the dark. And he stayed just long enough to try and impregnate me. That was his pattern. Once I became pregnant, he never came back. There was never any real affection between us."

"It sounds to me like you and Savea were like pieces on a game board," commented Tamara. "After father was born, how much interaction did you have with grandfather?"

"Almost none. There were a few State occasions, but that

was all," Solange remarked.

"And I spent the entire time from your father's birth until just recently in a lava dwelling that I built near the volcano. My feelings were so raw and my anger so intense that I couldn't seem to move beyond those emotions," cried Savea. "Solange, I'm so sorry."

Solange hugged her sister and said softly, "Savea, you were under a spell. You did nothing intentionally. And when you consider what was going on with the clarity of thought that we now have, that spell kept us apart so that we could not think clearly and unite our powers against what was happening."

Tamara added, "I think we have moved our problem-solving from the possible to the probable. What question should we address next?"

"We haven't quite finished our present analysis. Who would most benefit from this deception and why?" asked Solange.

"We touched on it earlier by proposing the Super Brothers as candidates," suggested Savea. "We may need to table that question for a bit while we think about the kidnapping of Tamara's family."

"What are some likely reasons for such a crime?" asked Tamara. "And why cover it up by creating a fake accident scenario?"

"The answer to your second question is obvious, I think," commented Solange. "The so-called accident would confuse any investigation. If it weren't for your earlier vision, we wouldn't know that your family is still alive."

Savea rose and turned back to the table. "I have an idea. Who would be most affected and influenced by the kidnapping? I'm pretty sure that would be you, Tamara. Even though our previous meeting with Sunan resulted in the hypothesis that Sostor was creating a weapon and kidnapped your family to force your father to identify weaknesses in our kingdom that could be exploited to produce an endgame of taking control of our crystals, there is another possibility. Your father and mother do not have any observable powers like ours, since those powers follow the female hereditary line that flows through Solange and me. Remember that your mother is a land dweller. And I assume your father is a carrier of the power, passed on to you at birth, but he probably has no innate power himself. We don't yet know what will transpire with Trina when she reaches puberty."

"Wait a minute," exclaimed Solange. "Didn't Sunan suggest that there was also a stream of power that flowed through the Super Brothers? He guessed that such a stream might move through the male lineage, just as ours moves through the female line."

"I'd forgotten about his conclusion," admitted Savea. "But it certainly makes sense that Sostor might be seeking to seize control of our crystals—which, combined with his own, would significantly dominate Sunan's single crystal. And it was the reason for Sunan's immediate return to Mesarra to ramp up his defenses. Have you heard from him since he left?"

Tamara shook her head and replied, "No, I haven't. But I do expect to hear soon. And I think all your assumptions are correct. But what else might the kidnapper want from me to warrant such horrible actions? Money? Influence? Favors?"

"Well, we know from your vision, Tamara, that your family is being held in Mosshire by Sostor. That would certainly make Sostor the number one suspect," offered Solange. "As to his motives, that should be the focus of our next discussion."

Chapter 7
Return of Sunan

"Your Majesty," cried a Page. "The Bubble Train has returned and Sunan is aboard!"

"Please notify the Sisters and ask them to meet Sunan and me in the Private Dining Room," ordered Tamara.

* * * * *

Tamara and Sunan entered the Private Dining Room and greeted the Sisters. Sunan bowed and said, "Thank you for welcoming me back. I understand that you have been working on a three-pronged approach to defending this kingdom. What have you accomplished so far?"

Savea began, "I directed lava into a channel that I have dug surrounding the kingdom. Then I vaporized lava to form a defensive dome over the kingdom that is designed to deter attack and yet allow the ocean to surround us. This is beyond physics and is controlled by my powers. Solange, please share what you have done."

"With my powers," added Solange, "I have used heat energy from the lava to create an underground tunnel that will accomplish two things: melt the solidified lava that lies beneath the ocean and immediately reapply it to fortify the tunnel walls to allow the Bubble Train to run safely beneath the ground.

"My personal concern is, of course, my son and his family. I'm hoping, Sunan, that we can partner to devise a strategy to free them from captivity."

"As for me," contributed Tamara, "I've been working with my crystals on both defensive and offensive moves. My crystals seem to activate and enable my new bracelets to both attack and defend."

"I'm truly impressed at what the three of you have accomplished," complimented Sunan. "As for me, I designed and built a dome as well. Mine will filter and redirect sunlight to repel any airborne attack while it also protects my citizens from harmful sun effects."

"What about when the sun isn't shining?" asked Tamara.

"I created an underground power source to support the primary power supply. While doing so, I also built a tunnel leading to the North. It goes all the way to the outer edge of Sostor's kingdom. From there, it will be relatively easy to keep tabs on what is going on. I can't give you more details since it is classified; just trust me, please," he implored.

"We do trust you, Sunan, or we wouldn't have shared our plans with you," assured Tamara. "But I do have some questions to ask you."

"Of course. Ask away," replied Sunan.

"Did you ever meet my grandfather or the king that preceded him?" Tamara began.

"Yes, I met them many years ago," Sunan responded. "I attended your grandfather's coronation."

"They were BOTH there?" asked Tamara. "Why was grandfather being elevated to King of Marinea if his father was still alive?"

"I don't know," Sunan answered. "I was wondering that myself."

Savea commented, "I didn't attend the coronation since I had moved to the volcano area and was nursing my sadness and anger at not being chosen to wed Tamara's grandfather."

"Actually, I wasn't there, either," said Solange. "The betrothal was not yet official and I was confined to my quarters."

"How strange," commented Tamara. "It's as if you were being prevented from noticing something that wasn't quite right."

"Now that you mention it," injected Sunan, "I was seated quite a distance from the coronation dais. The only persons actually on the dais were the exiting and incoming kings. Everyone else was quite a distance away and the lights were low."

"This supports our suspicions that the two kings were artificially created and not real beings. What do you think of that possibility?" asked Tamara.

"I have never considered such a possibility, but now I question what I believed I saw that day," concluded Sunan. "Thinking back, there did seem to be a slight distortion around the two figures, which I assumed at the time was a trick of the lighting. Now I think that you may be right."

"And after that ceremony," prompted Solange, "What became of the two kings?"

"The exiting king left the stage and I never saw him again," replied Sunan. "The newly crowned king sat on the throne and the audience was ushered out of the room. I later heard that he was ill and the next time he appeared in public was at your Royal Wedding."

Solange exclaimed, "It was right after the coronation that we were hastily married in a private ceremony. The official Royal Wedding took place later.

"And our wedding night was also odd. The lights in my bedroom were quite dim. A scarf was tied over my eyes and I was told it was tradition. After our physical union, I heard the door close and I found myself alone."

"At what point did you discover that you were with child," asked Savea.

"It was a few months later and we only had limited physical contact after that first night. He seemed to know when I was fertile," replied Solange. "Once I knew I was with child, I was informed that the King was ill and had gone abroad for treatment."

"I have another theory to add to this scenario," offered Sunan. "I'm embarrassed to even suggest it, but I will. If the two kings were holograms or androids or some other artificial entities, couldn't it be possible—given that you were actually blindfolded on your wedding night—that another person might have been with you that night?"

Solange gasped and cried out, "Are you suggesting that Trident's father was not the king?"

"I'm afraid I am," responded Sunan, "And whoever was his father might be the person behind the entire scheme. I'd like to help you retrieve any memories that you might have of that night. Would that be acceptable to you?"

"Of course," agreed Solange. "We need to get to the bottom of this."

"Then I'm going to put you in a light state of hypnosis. You will remember everything that you or I say. There will be no secrets. Now please sit down and relax in your chair. Close your eyes and breathe deeply."

Solange took a seat and followed Sunan's instructions. As

she relaxed, Sunan raised his hands and a shower of golden haze covered her.

"Solange, I am going to help you access your various senses to enhance your memories. First, let's consider sight. You told us that your eyes were covered by a scarf. Do you remember who did that?" asked Sunan.

"Yes," she responded. "Although the lights were very low, a member of the king's personal guard came toward me and tied the scarf over my eyes."

"Would you be able to recognize that guard?" asked Sunan.

"I'm not sure," she replied. "It all happened so fast, and the lights were so dim."

"Was the king present in the room?" Sunan pressed.

"I believe that he was near the door," she said.

"Could you see him clearly?" asked Sunan.

"No, his image was somewhat indistinct. I wondered about that," Solange added.

Sunan shifted his line of questioning to another sense. "Now please think about sound. Can you remember any sounds that were occurring at that time?"

"I could hear a clock ticking in the corner. At some point, the clock chimed eleven times."

"Did it chime again during your time together?" asked

Sunan.

"Yes. I heard twelve chimes and then one," she responded.

"So can we agree that you and the king were together for at least two hours?"

"Yes, I think that would be correct," Solange agreed.

"Consider now the sense of smell," directed Sunan. "Can you describe the odors that were present in your previous interactions with the king?"

"He was partial to a cologne that smelled a bit like chemicals," she replied.

"And was that smell present on your wedding night?" asked Sunan.

"It was at the beginning. But after my eyes were bound by the scarf, I didn't smell it anymore. When we were making love, I could smell a different scent, somewhat woodsy, like a forest," Solange responded.

"I'd like to consider taste now," said Sunan. "When you kissed, was there any identifiable taste present?"

"Definitely," Solange recalled. "It was a minty taste like I've encountered before in mouthwash or breath mints."

"Now let's talk about touch," Sunan suggested. "What can you remember about the king's touch?"

"When we were courting, he never touched me. I was told that was inappropriate until we were wed. In fact, whenever we went anywhere, we rode in separate vehicles," she remembered.

"Didn't you wonder about that? His behavior doesn't sound very romantic. What was it that drew you to him and made you agree to marry him?" asked Sunan.

"I don't know," she wept. "When I look back at it, none of it makes sense to me."

"Let's return to your wedding night," said Sunan. "What was his touch like during your lovemaking?"

"It was gentle and yet stimulating. I felt myself responding to it with great joy and pleasure. When he left the room, I became depressed and saddened," she answered. "It was a sense of abandonment. In many ways, during the years of raising my son, I was challenged almost every day to rise above the negative aspects of my marriage in order to give light and joy to my son."

Savea put her arms around her Sister and tears spilled from her eyes. "I'm so sorry I wasn't there for you, Solange."

Sunan raised his arms and the golden haze dissipated. "I think we have a lot of memories to discuss. You may awaken now, Solange, and you will remember everything."

Solange opened her eyes and returned Savea's hug. "Please don't cry, my dear. It was the spell that bound us. Now we must share our interpretations of my memories."

Chapter 8
From Conjecture to Evidence

The Sisters, Sunan and Tamara moved to an area of the Private Dining Room that had couches along one wall. Making themselves comfortable, the three women looked to Sunan to begin the discussion. "Please take the lead on this, Sunan," Solange asked. "You were in charge of the hypnosis experiment."

"Let's take each sense one by one," Sunan suggested. "But before we begin, I want to ask you, Solange, if the experience of analyzing the senses confirmed any of your suspicions. Just answer 'yes' or 'no' please. I don't want to influence the others at this point."

"I'd have to say somewhat, but not definitely," she replied.

"Fair enough," said Sunan. "Then let's begin with 'sight'. You told us that the light was dim in the room and that the king was a distance away by the door. You added that what you did see of him was 'indistinct'. Do you want to add anything else to that description?"

"No. That sums up my visual memory," concluded Solange. "Oh, wait a minute. There was also that guard in the room, the one that tied the scarf around my eyes."

"Did he remain in the room?" asked Savea.

"Since my eyes were covered, I didn't actually see him leave. But I did hear the door close," replied Solange.

"So at least one person left the room—but it could have been more," commented Tamara.

"That's true. I never thought of that," Solange admitted.

"That moves us nicely into 'sound'," said Sunan. "The only sound you identified were the chimes of the clock. Upon reflection, were any other sounds present?"

"Well, I did just mention the closing of the door. Other than that, I don't remember anything but the king coming to my bed and the sound of his lying down next to me."

"Which leads us to 'smell'," added Sunan. "When did you notice a change in a recognizable smell?"

"I noticed it right away. I love the scent of mint," offered Solange. "His breath was quite delightful, not at all like the chemical small I was used to."

"What about the woodsy smell you reported earlier? Was that present?" asked Sunan.

"Oh yes, I'm sorry I forgot to mention it," affirmed Solange.

"Interesting," observed Sunan, "And that leads us quite nicely to 'taste'. I see a definite link between 'smell' and 'taste' in that you described the taste of his kiss as 'minty'."

"I agree," commented Tamara. "My assessment is that it was a strong link, too strong to be natural. I suspect that it came from heavy use of mouthwash or breath mints, as you mentioned earlier, Solange."

"Do you remember anything else related to either 'smell' or 'taste'," asked Savea.

"I don't," answered Solange. "I guess that just leaves us with 'touch'."

"Your wedding night seems to have produced some delightful memories related to 'touch'," Savea remarked. "Until the king abruptly left you, that is."

"Very true, and I clung to those memories for many years," agreed Solange. "They helped to keep me sane while I worked hard to move past the negative aspects of my marriage."

"I am going to propose to you that we now have a scenario that is no longer based entirely on conjecture," argued Sunan. "By creating a framework based on the five senses, I think we have added a significant amount of real evidence."

"So the scenario that I see," determined Savea, "Is one in which a spell was cast that obscured the true natures of the prior king and his son, Tamara's supposed grandfather. And neither of them was an actual living being. I believe that spell was designed to create false beliefs in our population and a rift between Solange and me. My sister and I were so affected that it separated us and we were unable to see what was happening. That spell had to have been incredibly powerful. Let's talk a bit about who or what could have cast it—and why?"

"And as a stakeholder who wasn't alive at that time, I'd also like to identify who might be my father's father. I think that this is a key question," added Tamara.

"Could we take a lunch break before we delve into these mysteries again?" asked Solange. "I feel overwhelmed at the moment."

"Of course," replied Tamara. "I'll send for some food immediately.

* * * * *

After finishing a delicious lunch of lobster and potatoes, all four amateur detectives returned to where they had paused their deliberations.

Once again seated comfortably on the couches, Sunan addressed the Sisters and Tamara, "If you would indulge me, I would like to try two approaches. The first one concerns confirming that Solange and Savea were so spellbound that it seriously affected their world view and approach to each other."

"How will we do that?" asked Savea.

"I know a spell that I would like Tamara to try, while holding hands with both of you. She has had a significant effect on you both before and I would like to try an experiment," urged Sunan. "Tamara, if you are willing, please walk with me for a few minutes while I share the contents of that spell with you."

Sunan and Tamara walked slowly across the room, conversing in low tones. When they returned to the Sisters, Tamara took their hands and began to slowly chant the spell Sunan had shared with her. The three women became surrounded by a silver haze that pulsed on and off. The crystals on Tamara's palms throbbed and sent a bright silver light up the arms of the Sisters to their heads. After a few minutes, the Sisters looked at each other in horror.

"What just happened?" asked Solange.

"I feel like I was transported back in time," cried Savea. "You and I were working on preparing a State Dinner to welcome the then king and his son back from an extensive trip abroad. When they arrived, there was a sudden undersea storm with a waterspout and visibility dropped to zero. The water currents were incredibly strong and we had to cling to nearby pillars to avoid being swept away. When the storm waned, everything had changed. I think that was when the spell was cast. I don't know who was responsible, but afterward our relationship was completely different and I felt a deep hatred for you. During the turmoil, the king and his son moved past us and headed to their rooms in the palace. Everything that happened after that is public knowledge. Did you have the same experience, Solange?"

"Yes, I did. Before that storm, we were loving sisters and close friends. Afterward, there was deep hostility between us and I didn't understand what had happened," affirmed Solange. "But suddenly I realized that I was betrothed to the king's son and I didn't remember ever agreeing to it."

"And I was so hurt and angry, leading to my decision to flee to the volcano area to live," added Savea.

"I was shocked to see that your beautiful white hair had turned jet black," remembered Solange.

"Thank you all for agreeing to this experiment," Sunan said with approval. "The chant I shared with Tamara was one that identifies when a spell is cast. So you are correct in your assumption that the time you just revisited contained the moment you became spellbound. Clearly, it was directly connected to the arrival of the king and his son. Was anyone with them when they reached the palace?"

"Yes, in my vision, there was a group of guards accompanying them, perhaps a dozen. Do you agree, Savea?"

asked Solange.

"I do. But I really didn't pay attention to them while I was clinging to the pillar for safety. Oddly, though, no one in that royal party seemed to be affected by the storm," commented Savea.

"Interesting," remarked Sunan. "Then it would appear that the so-called storm was directed at the two of you and was a diversion to keep you from focusing on the king and his son. As both of you agree on what Tamara's chant has illuminated, I conclude that we have moved from conjecture to evidence. Would you like to rest for a while and can we meet back here in about three hours? In the meantime, please take notes about any dreams or visions you may experience."

Tamara and the Sisters agreed to Sunan's suggestion and left the room to take a must-needed break.

Chapter 9
An Unanticipated Twist

Three hours later, Tamara and the Sisters reconvened with Sunan in the Private Dining Room. Only Tamara returned with some notes to share. "I had a dream that I was there when the king and his son walked through the storm to the palace. In my dream, they were encased in bubbles that kept them dry and not affected by the wind and waves. The guards that accompanied them were also unaffected. The Sisters were clinging desperately to the pillars, unaware of anything but the storm and its effects. It was quite strange."

"Did anyone beside the king and his son grab your attention in the dream?" asked Sunan.

"Yes," responded Tamara. "There was one guard who seemed to be in charge. He followed the king closely and kept sprinkling everyone in the party with silver glitter. Occasionally, a member of the party would begin to fade, but came back into sharp focus once sprinkled with the glitter. It was very confusing,"

"It doesn't surprise me that you are the only one to have a dream or vision," commented Sunan. "The Sisters were intimately involved in what was happening; you were not yet born. Does your dream suggest anything to you?"

"My first thought was that I was watching a spell in action," she answered. "And I never saw the head guard sprinkle himself, so I concluded that he was real and no one else in the royal party was."

"Very perceptive," Sunan pronounced. "Can you describe the appearance of this head guard?"

"I'm afraid not," admitted Tamara. "His face was turned away from me and he was wearing a hood and long sleeves and pants, so I don't even know the color of his hair or skin."

"I would call that a very clever disguise by someone who had calculated carefully," offered Savea.

Sunan turned to the Sisters and asked, "Do either of you have anything to add? If not, as I mentioned earlier, there are two approaches that I would like to try. We completed the first one, and now, with your permission, I would like to try the second one."

"Will it take long?" asked Tamara. "If so, as we are approaching the dinner hour, I should inform the chef that we will be delayed."

"I am not certain," responded Sunan. "Would you prefer to wait until after dinner?"

"I believe so," answered Tamara. "I think we would all be more comfortable. I will request that our dinner be served."

* * * * *

After dinner, as they lingered over dessert, Tamara briought up Sunan's second approach. Please introduce this idea of yours," Tamara urged.

"Thank you for allowing me this latitude," Sunan said. "I know it will defer our larger discussion until tomorrow, but I have a strong suspicion that the outcome will be informative.

"You are aware that the Sisters and I are three of the four Super Children, Sostor being the fourth. I believe that the Sisters have been important pawns in an ongoing game, unwitting participants in a long-range bid for power. It is so meaningful to me that you have chosen to trust me when I have not as yet earned that trust.

"I wish to undertake a second experiment, this time with Tamara. While the three of us have a lot of power, I believe that Tamara's emerging power is significantly greater."

Tamara looked at Sunan in shock. "Are you serious? As Super Children, you three are incredibly powerful!"

"I agree, but let's not underestimate your capabilities, Tamara."

"What I would like to try has never been done before," Sunan pronounced. "With the Sisters as observers, I would like to take your hands, Tamara, and have you chant that spell I shared with you once again. Then we will see what happens."

Tamara looked at the Sisters inquiringly. "What do you think?" she asked.

"I believe it would be an interesting experiment," replied Solange. "Savea and I will be here to keep you safe."

"And I foresee that the outcome will surprise us all," added Savea. "Be safe, my dear ones."

With the unanimous support of the Sisters, Tamara and Sunan stood and clasped hands. Tamara began to chant the spell, first softly and then louder.

As before, with the Sisters, a silver haze moved from the crystals on her palms up Sunan's arms to his head. But this time, the haze began to revolve and became a silver tornado that lifted of them both into the air. As the two spun faster and faster, the Sisters gasped. Rising to her feet, Solange cried, "What shall we do?" Savea put her hand on her Sister's arm, pulled her back to sit on the couch and spoke soothingly, "Let them be," she urged. "I have a good feeling about this."

The crystal on Tamara's forehead began to shoot rainbows around the room. Slowly, the two descended to the floor and Sunan helped Tamara over to one of the couches. As they sat, Sunan lovingly took Tamara's hands and kissed her cheek. "Sunan," cried Tamara, "YOU are my grandfather!"

"So it seems, my dear," he replied. "I suspected that I might have also been spelled and we just found out that I was correct."

"Sunan, YOU were my lover on my wedding night?" accused Solange.

Moving to Solange's side, Sunan put his arm around her shoulders and spoke softly, "Tamara broke the spell that has had me bound for so many years. I can now remember that night clearly—and with great love, although I couldn't feel it at the time. My dear, I hope you will forgive my spell-induced behavior on your wedding night. I apologize for any untoward actions that I may have committed that night."

Solange smiled and put her hand on his. "Actually, your behavior was stimulating!" she teased. Blushing, she added, "I hope we'll have an opportunity to get to know each other better—but this revelation complicates matters, my Brother," Solange mused aloud. "By the time we figure all of this out, I may discover I've always been single!"

Turning to Savea, she asked, "Savea, did you know this was coming?"

"I had a suspicion," Savea answered. "Although the storm forced me to cling to the pillar, I was able to turn slightly and catch a glimpse of another guard who remained clear and in focus throughout the passage into the palace. Although it didn't register with me at the time, it kept tugging at my memory of that day. Eventually, it was buried in the anger I felt after what I interpreted as your betrayal. After our spell was broken, I began to think that mysterious guard might be Sunan. But I wasn't sure until now."

"I'm so excited," cried Tamara. "I have a living grandfather!"

Solange smiled, "And just think of your father's reaction when we tell him the news!"

Chapter 10
Attention to the Three-Pronged Plan

When they next convened, Tamara resumed the discussion with a reminder: "Remember that we still need to discuss the three-pronged plan we designed to protect the kingdom: a safer, underground route for the Bubble Train; a rescue of my family from Sostor; and analysis of the powers available to me through my crystals and bracelets. Which of these approaches should we focus on first?"

Solange asserted, "My preference would be, of course, to commence with the rescue of my son and his family. But I also understand that we had better reconfigure our defenses first so that we have more leverage. Tamara, I acknowledge that your powers are important and are growing more significant with each passing day, but could we start by talking about the Bubble Train?"

"Of course, Grandmother," acknowledged Tamara. "You and Savea have created an impressive tunnel design utilizing lava as a protective material. Where are you in implementing that project?"

Savea responded, "It has already been completed. Solange and I make a formidable team when we join forces."

"That's wonderful," exclaimed Tamara. "And what about the dome over the kingdom? That was to be a lava project, too."

"Also in place," offered Solange. "Both projects were completed before our recent efforts at removing spells."

"And, Sunan, where are you in establishing your defenses?" asked Tamara.

"As I mentioned when I arrived, I authorized and built the new defenses to be constructed. I am satisfied that they will hold against most attacks. At least, I am hopeful," he added.

Tamara clapped her hands. "I am pleased and relieved. Not only has one prong of our plan been accomplished, but your similar project has been as well. What should we tackle next?"

Sunan stood and walked over to Solange. "While I understand the importance of creating a rescue plan, I believe that the exploration of Tamara's powers is critical to a positive result. Remember that she has two strands of power: one from the female side through you Sisters and one from the male side from me and her father. "

Solange added, "We don't know yet just how powerful she is and might grow to be. But I feel certain that we will need her help to successfully rescue my son and his family."

"I agree," declared Savea. "We need every arrow in our quiver of power if we are to defeat Sostor. He is a very clever sorcerer and not to be underestimated. But are you certain that Tamara's father has power?"

"Absolutely. He may not yet be aware of it or understand how to control it. But that is a project for another day," affirmed Sunan.

Solange sighed, "I understand what you are saying and also agree that we need to have all possible resources at our disposal. I hope we can quickly accomplish this daunting task of understanding Tamara's power potential. I'm so worried and afraid of what Sostor might do."

Sunan turned to Tamara, "Would you please summarize what you know of your powers for me? I was certainly impressed by how the spell binding me was broken."

Tamara looked at the Sisters and implored, "Please assist me in trying to remember everything. You both have been so helpful to me as I work to understand my powers so far."

"Of course, my dear," replied Solange. "Why don't you begin with your crystals: their location and what has taken place since they became activated?"

Tamara nodded her head and began to apprise Sunan of what they had learned. "I was born with a crystal on my stomach. It did not activate—by which I mean change colors—until I reached puberty. The Sisters helped me to realize that it was reflecting my emotions. My hair also began changing color.

"Then the day after my coronation, crystals appeared on my palms and forehead. They haven't changed color, but the ones on my palms were able to extinguish Solange's robe when it accidentally caught fire. Right after that, the Sisters asked me to practice moving and blowing up candles—and I was successful doing both. So we determined that those crystals had both defensive and offensive powers."

Savea added, "There was also the time that Tamara fainted in the Chapel. Dr. Astarte, the Court Physician, asked for our help. While Tamara was lying on her bed, Solange and I were softly chanting a spell and suddenly Tamara levitated. Her forehead crystal turned from white to silver and shot rays to her wrists, forming bracelets. She has been unable to remove those bracelets ever since and after she sank back down on her bed, the crystal returned to a white color."

Tamara burst in excitedly, "Then there was the time when I was in my bath and fell asleep, slipping down into the water. I don't know why my gills didn't save me. What happened was that my bracelets pulled my arms into the air and levitated me over to my bed, where I continued to sleep."

"Well, that's a lot to absorb," commented Sunan. "I think you should continue your exercises, both physical and emotional. Was Dr. Astarte consulted about this last incident?"

"Yes," answered Solange. "She had some tests done and discovered there is a marker in Tamara's blood that is also present in my blood and Savea's. Dr. Astarte thinks it's gender-related since my son does not have it. But in order for Tamara to have it, the marker must have come through Trident since her mother is a non-magical. He must be a carrier."

Sunan requested, "I'd like to have tests done on my blood and compared with Trident's. His blood tests should be on file. I suspect that a second marker exists that is male-related. Then I'd like to know if Tamara also has that marker."

Solange suggested, "I'd recommend that we postpone discussing the idea of a ball until we unravel some of these new questions."

"I concur," Savea said. "I'll stay here and help Tamara with her exercises. When the tests are complete, let's meet back here in the Private Dining Room."

Chapter 11
More Evidence to Consider

It was almost dinnertime the following day when the four reconvened in the Private Dining Room. Almost immediately, Dr. Astarte entered the room with a handful of files.

"What do your tests show, Doctor? Was Sunan correct in his suspicions?" asked Tamara.

"Yes, Your Majesty, he was," replied the Doctor. "There is a second marker. It was difficult to locate as it is completely different than the one we found before. It obviously follows the male line and Trident has it as well. What is even more interesting is that Tamara also has that marker."

"I knew it!" exclaimed Sunan. "That's why she is so powerful. She is channeling both power streams. How unique! Do you think this accounts for her crystals?"

Dr. Astarte answered, "That is as yet undetermined. I'm going to consult with my colleague, Dr. Angelus. He has a degree in magical sciences and may have some ideas about that." Turning to leave, she added, "I'll get back to you as soon as I can."

"So, to summarize what we have learned," offered Tamaara, "My original crystal and my hair reflect my emotions. The crystals on my palms can be both defensive and offensive. My forehead crystal and the bracelets that it formed are protective. Am I correct?"

"Those are my conclusions, too—so far," agreed Sunan. "I believe much more will be revealed through time and experience."

"I'd like to return to the idea of having a ball," proposed Solange. "We know so much more than we did during your and Sostor's last visit. As much as I hate to say this, I don't think the time is ripe for Savea to go to Mosshire and attempt to save my son and his family. We need to study Sostor and try to gain intel through clever questioning and a social occasion would be ideal for such an endeavor. But I think Sostor would notice Savea's absence and be on guard."

"Knowing what I do of my brother's thinking, I agree with your logic," admitted Sunan. "But I don't want to push the rescue mission too far into the future. Tamara, how soon do you think a ball could be scheduled?"

"Can we think of a good reason for having a ball?" asked Savea.

"How about my birthday?" suggested Tamara. "I will turn twenty in a couple of weeks. It doesn't have to be on the exact date."

"That's brilliant!" Solange exclaimed, "But we must

maintain secrecy regarding what we discovered about each other after the spells were broken. Sostor must not find out that we know the truth about Sunan. He must continue to believe that the status quo of two females vs. two males in the quartet of Super Beings is still intact."

"I totally agree," said Sunan. "Otherwise he would feel threatened and I don't know what he would do."

"And Sunan, you must pretend that you have just arrived. Your extended visit here must remain a secret," Tamara stressed. "I'll inform the staff of the importance of this."

"Now that we're agreed on the next step," said Savea, "I'm starving! Let's have dinner!"

* * * * *

The next day, invitations to Tamara's birthday ball were sent to Sostor and a selection of friends and acquaintances from Marinea and the mainland. An extra Bubble Train was scheduled to accommodate the increased number of riders. The date of the ball was only three weeks away, so much had to be done in a short period of time.

One week later, no response had yet been received from Sostor and Tamara was worried. She met with the Sisters and Sunan and expressed her concern. Sunan offered to contact his brother, but hesitated to do so because they had not been on speaking terms for some time. Savea suggested that he might ask Sostor if he was planning to attend the ball and, if so, could they arrange some time to have a private meeting. Sunan agree to do so and hoped that Sostor would be sufficiently curious about the proposed meeting to send a positive RSVP.

Two weeks later, Sunan reported that Sostor had agreed to meet with him at the ball. Tamara affirmed that she had received a positive response from Sostor. Their plan appeared to be on track. It was now time to work out the details.

* * * * *

Tamara and the Sisters were chatting when Sunan entered the Private Dining Room. "Sunan, we were discussing possible strategies for gaining intel from Sostor," said Tamara. "I suggested presenting myself as a distraught daughter asking for his help in locating my family. What do you think?"

Sunan nodded and agreed, "That sounds logical and possibly may be persuasive. Certainly he won't confess to having taken them, but perhaps his response will have some clues for us. Solange, what approach will you use?"

"I thought I'd try to appeal to our shared status as Super Children and ask if he had any ideas about how to find my son and his family. Do you think he would be receptive to that?"

"It would definitely appeal to his ego," Sunan answered.

"I think he would be pleased if you acknowledged his importance as a Super Being."

"I thought I would stroke his ego even more by effusively praising him for coming to Tamara's ball and saying how honored she must feel that he would do so. I decided against asking favors and exhibiting emotion. However, I might hint at a continuing friction between Solange and me. I want him to see me as a possible ally," Savea added.

"That's brilliant," Sunan approved. "You might be able to penetrate a whole other part of his character. As for me, in the private meeting that I asked for, I intend to try to relate to him as a brother and investigate ways to mend our fences. I don't know if that will work, but I can play the role of a supplicant role pretty well. I believe he would feel more powerful as a result."

Tamara clapped her hands and smiled. "Those are four very different angles. I love our creativity! Let's agree that we will play our roles individually and not approach him together."

Sunan nodded agreement, as did the Sisters. "Then I think we have a workable plan," said Tamara. "I hope nothing raises Sostor's suspicions. After the ball is over, we need to meet as soon as possible to compare intel and impressions. Our mission after that will be to design a rescue plan."

Chapter 12
The Ball

Tamara stood at her bedroom mirror and gazed approvingly at her image. *I think this dress is perfect*, she thought.

Her personal attendant entered the room and clapped her hands. "Your Majesty, you look beautiful!" Mia gushed. "That emerald color really suits you. And I love the little stars embroidered all over it. Are you ready for me to do your hair now?

"Yes, Mia," she answered. "Do you know if any guests have yet arrived?"

"The Bubble Train has just arrived, so the first ones are probably here," Mia said.

"If you hear that Sostor was on that train, please let me know," Tamara requested. "I want to greet him as soon as possible."

Mia agreed and proceeded to arrange Tamara's hair.

* * * * *

Tamara was putting the finishing touches on her makeup when Mia gently knocked at the door. "Come in," Tamara called. Mia rushed in and informed Tamara that Sostor had indeed been on that first Bubble Train and was now being escorted to the Ballroom. Tamara thanked her and hurried to the door. Walking gracefully down the hall, she soon arrived at the Ballroom.

"Good evening, My Lord," she welcomed Sostor. "I'm pleased that we will have a few moments to converse before many guests have arrived."

"I, too, appreciate the opportunity to get to know you better," replied Sostor suavely. "I'm afraid that our last encounter ended rather abruptly. I apologize for letting my temper flare. I often react that way when challenged."

"I'm sorry that you felt challenged, My Lord," soothed Tamara. "As I recall that conversation, we were merely expressing interest and curiosity. Since we did not know each other well, our questions were meant to illuminate, not intrude. My apologies if you interpreted them differently."

"Nicely said, Your Majesty," responded Sostor with a slight sneer on his face. "Your political skills are impressive."

"I hope that you can recognize sincerity in my words, my Lord," implored Tamara. "I have been so upset in recent weeks, since my family boarded the Bubble Train to the mainland and were never seen again. I love them deeply and not a day passes that I am not grieving."

Sostor took Tamara's hand and kissed it, saying, "My sympathies, Your Majesty. I can understand your sadness."

Tamara froze and lowered her eyes so that Sostor could not see her reaction. She struggled to control; her emotions so that her crystals would not alert him to her feelings. Sostor's touch, however, was revealing. While she could not exactly read his mind, she could identify waves of intent and purpose when his hand touched the crystal on her palm. She had never responded to anyone like this before. Certainly, another attribute of one of her crystals had identified itself.

Intensely interested in further exploring this new phenomenon, she covered his hand with her other palm. Instantly, images flooded her mind. She once again saw her family in Mosshire, thinner than she remembered and looking unhappy. She received accompanying emotions from Sostor of greed, intent to deceive and force compliance, desire to control and manipulate, and an ultimate belief that perceived enemies should be eliminated. There was little hope or charity in what she observed. Bracing herself, she took Sostor's arm and, together, they walked across the Ballroom to mingle with some of the guests.

*   *   *   *   *

Solange walked up to where Tamara and Sostor stood

talking. She welcomed Sostor by saying, "My Lord, how nice to see you again. I am so pleased that you could spare the time to attend Tamara's birthday ball."

"I hadn't realized it was her birthday until I received the invitation," replied Sostor. "Happy Birthday, Your Majesty."

"Thank you, my Lord. Now many guests have arrived and I must take my leave to welcome them. Please excuse me. I hope to continue our conversation later," Tamara demurred and walked away to chat with new arrivals.

"She has grown into an enchanting young woman," commented Sostor. "Are suitors lining up to woo her?" he asked.

"I don't pry into her private life," Solange asserted. "What I do know is that she is an excellent ruler of this kingdom. That responsibility was thrust upon her so suddenly when my son and the rest of the family disappeared in that Bubble Train accident. I assume you heard of it, am I correct?"

"Yes, of course. It was widely broadcast at the time," answered Sostor. "Has any information come to light about the cause of the accident?"

"Very little," responded Solange. "I was wondering if I could enlist your assistance in seeking answers? Since we are both Super Children, I thought perhaps joining forces with you might uncover some information that has so far been overlooked. Would you be interested in helping me launch an investigation?"

"I would certainly like to do so," he answered, "But our kingdoms are so far apart and my responsibilities take up most of my time. However, if you would like me to assist you in analyzing any intel that you discover, we could do that using a vid link."

"I'm sure that any assistance you could offer would be helpful, My Lord," she assured him. "Do you have any suggestions as to how I might begin my quest?" she questioned.

"I will think it over and try to come up with some options," he promised. "I'll get back to you as soon as I can."

"Thank you," Solange purred. "Now I must return to welcoming the guests. Please excuse me," she added as she walked away.

* * * * *

Savea watched Solange leave Sostor and decided that the time was perfect to put her strategy into action. Moving quickly through the throng of guests, she reached him in a matter of minutes. "Good evening, Sostor," she said with a smile. "I am so delighted that you were able to join us. It's an honor to have you with us—all four Super Children in one place celebrating a family birthday!"

Sostor looked at her skeptically. "All four? Is Sunan expected as well?"

"Oh yes," she affirmed. "He has just arrived and should join the festivities soon. Do you Brothers have much opportunity to get together? I imagine it's more difficult for you, having different kingdoms to govern. Solange and I live in closer proximity—not that easy access necessarily makes our relationship any better."

"I had heard that the two of you were not on the best of terms," offered Sostor. "Are things any better now?" he probed.

"I'm sure you are familiar with the challenges siblings face—particularly siblings of the same gender. We try, but our success rate is variable," added Savea.

"I'm sorry to hear that," said Sostor. "If you are looking for a sibling who might understand, I can offer myself as a sounding board."

"I appreciate that, Sostor," Savea contributed. "I may take you up on that. And it would be wonderful to get to know each other better."

"We could begin by enjoying the music that just started," invited Sostor. "Would you like to dance?"

* * * * *

Sunan entered the Ballroom in time to notice Sostor's invitation to dance. Smiling to himself, he walked to the doorway to the garden and took a seat where he could easily observe the room.

Sostor twirled Savea and, while doing so, spotted Sunan sitting by the garden door. As the music stopped, he bowed to Savea and said, "Thank you for the dance. I hope we have another opportunity this evening," and turned to walk toward Sunan. Savea watched him leave, a smile of triumph on her face.

As Sostor, neared him, Sunan stood and extended his hand in greeting. "It's so nice to see you, Brother. I hope that we will find some time to catch up."

"Actually, this might be a good opportunity. Shall we take a walk in the garden?" proposed Sostor.

"That's an excellent idea," Sunan agreed as he turned to enter the garden. Sostor followed him out the door.

"What did you want to talk about?" asked Sostor.

"We have grown apart, Brother, and I would like to try and mend any fences that separate us," replied Sunan. "After all, you and I were once a single Being. Surely we can repair any ill feelings we might have."

"Frankly, I think of us more as competitors than collaborators," Sostor asserted.

"But why?" asked Sunan. "Our kingdoms are far apart so there is no reason to compete. In fact, if we were to work together to improve our kingdoms, both would benefit. Won't you at least consider such a working arrangement?"

"You're being ridiculous, Brother," claimed Sostor. "My kingdom is so much more prosperous than yours. The people you govern are like lotus-eaters, living in a dream world and consumed with enjoying life. They have little ambition and do not try to win. Why would I want to spend my resources helping such a lazy population?"

"Please, Brother," pleaded Sunan, "Our peoples could learn much from each other precisely because they have different values. Why are you being so hard-hearted?"

"I have great plans," replied Sostor, "And they don't include diverting my limited resources to any purpose other than what would benefit my own kingdom. You are a fool if you think otherwise. If that is all you wanted to talk about, this conversation is over." he snarled, stalking away.

As Sunan watched his Brother march back to the Ballroom, he smiled to himself. *"Great plans, he said. That bears a closer look."*

* * * * *

The next morning, Tamara, the Sisters, and Sunan

gathered together in the Private Dining Room to share what they had learned at the ball the night before. Tamara spoke first, "When I was sharing my 'grief' with Sostor, he kissed my hand and, while I could not accurately read his mind, I could feel intent and purpose as his hand touched the crystal on my palm. That had never happened to me before and I believe another power from my crystals has shown itself."

"That is a significant discovery," said Solange. "What intent and purpose did you identify?"

"I could sense manipulation and evasiveness, and an unwillingness to be honest or share. There was also hostility and greed—and a faint strand that I could not decipher. He has a dark soul. I just froze and it was very difficult to control my emotions—and therefore my hair and crystal colors—so that he would not be made aware of my powers. But I believe I managed it," Tamara added.

"So now we know your palm crystals can 'read' people. That's a very special skill," Savea commented. "We can certainly use it to our advantage. Solange, how did your encounter go?"

Solange replied, "As I had planned, I appealed to our shared Super Being status. Then I added a layer of worry about my son and his family. I asked whether he would be willing to assist me in searching for them. He said he was willing, but his kingdom was far away and his time was totally devoted to it. He suggested I contact him with any intel I gathered and he would help me analyze it!"

"A clever way to monitor what you know," commented Sunan.

"Yes, but also an inroad that would give us a path to spread disinformation," added Solange. "So I don't consider it a total waste of time."

"I agree," said Savea. "We are at least as clever as Sostor thinks he is. We now have an opportunity to manipulate him from afar."

Solange continued, "He also tried to elicit information from me, which I deflected. AND he seemed interested in Tamara's potential suitors!"

"What?" exclaimed Tamara. "How is that any of his business? However, let's not close that door entirely. It may be another possible inroad into his machinations."

"And I think I created another one," added Savea. "I gushed ego-building praise all over him, thanking him profusely for coming to your birthday ball. I also laid some tantalizing groundwork about our relationship, Solange, and hinted at possible fractures that he might see as opportunities to sow dissent between us. I was surprised when he asked me to dance, but I took it as a sign that my strategy was working.

Although I don't have the ability to intuit another person's intentions, I got the impression that Sostor has layers of personality that are still unknown to us. Sunan, how did you fare?"

"We went out into the garden for a walk," reported Sunan. "I tried to appeal to him by citing our shared origin as a single Super Being. I pleaded with him to consider working together to benefit both our kingdoms, but he brushed that off, telling me, as he did Solange, how busy he was governing his own kingdom. He specifically rejected sharing any resources and mentioned that he had 'great plans'. I see that as an avenue to be pursued; we need to discover what he is up to."

"Absolutely," agreed Tamara. "We have much to digest and I recommend that we meet again for breakfast tomorrow morning to chart some directions to take next. Sunan, when do you have to return to your kingdom?"

"My staff will keep it running smoothly in my absence," he responded. "I can remain until we have firm plans in place."

"That's wonderful," Tamara said appreciatively. "Then I'll see you all tomorrow morning."

Chapter 13
More Plotting and Planning

Tamara met the Sisters in the Private Dining Room early the next morning. Sunan had not yet arrived. Tamara took the Sisters' hands and asked, "Can I speak with you in confidence?"

"Of course," they agreed and the three women went to a couch and sat down.

"I want to touch both Brothers again," said Tamara. "I have a sense that there is more to discover in each of them than we are seeing. For example, both Savea and I could sense something hidden in Sostor and I'm troubled by what I cannot perceive in Sunan. We have trusted Sunan completely and confided much about our lives and kingdom to him. I'm not sure that was wise. Could we agree to be more circumspect about what we share, except with each other?"

"I think that would be prudent," agreed Solange. "We need to remember that, like Savea and me, they were once one Super Being and we don't know all the particulars of their division. On the surface, Sostor is cold, calculating and remote and Sunan is warm and approachable. Is that really accurate or is something else in play?"

At that point, Sunan entered the room and the women dropped that line of conversation. "Good morning, Sunan," welcomed Tamara. "I hope you had a good night's rest."

"Indeed I did," he replied. "How shall we resume our deliberations?"

"I've been pondering that," answered Tamara, "And I believe that we need to return to a discussion of our defenses. Sunan, have you been in contact with your staff to check on how your defense plan is being implemented?"

"I have not," he answered. "I was intending to do so later this morning when we take a break."

"Then let's begin with breakfast," suggested Tamara. "The three of us also need to check on preparations and we can do so after we have eaten. We can meet again after lunch."

As she stood and moved toward the breakfast table, she took Sunan's arm and placed her palm lightly on his forearm. Trying not to visibly react, she walked slowly with him and took her place at the table.

*   *   *   *   *

After breakfast, everyone left separately to check on preparations. However, Tamara and the Sisters had secretly arranged to gather in Tamara's bedroom to continue their previous conversation. Savea closed the door quietly and asked

Tamara, "I saw you take Sunan's arm. What did you learn?"

"He is hiding something. I picked up on elements of shame, regret and deceit. I don't know what to make of it," answered Tamara. "Is Sostor still in our kingdom or has he left?"

"I believe he is still here," said Solange. "Shall I send him an invitation to a private lunch?"

"If you don't mind," interrupted Savea. "With the groundwork that I've laid, I would prefer to issue that invitation myself and see what ensues."

"That's fine," replied Solange. "And if you agree, I will invite Sunan to have lunch with me on the terrace outside the Ballroom."

"While you two continue your investigations," sighed Tamara, "I think I will stay here and rest a bit before having lunch delivered to me here. When we gather again in the Private Dining Room, please make sure both Brothers accompany you. I'd like to read them one more time."

"What will you use as a pretext for that meeting?" asked Solange.

"A special dessert that I will have the Chef prepare for the four of us before the Brothers depart," suggested Tamara. "Shall we say 2:00?"

* * * * *

At precisely 2:00, Tamara and the Chef arrived at the Private Dining Room to greet the others. With a flourish, the Chef produced a tray with four dishes of cake and ice cream and placed it on the table. "This is a treat that the Chef has created for us. Thank you, Chef, for your efforts," gushed Tamara.

Tamara and the Chef served each of the Brothers first, Tamara making sure that she touched their hands in the process. She pretended to lose her balance when she came to Sostor and apologized for her clumsiness. Turning to Sunan, after handing him his dish, she led him to a table and sat next to him while the Chef served her and the Sisters.

After savoring the delicious dessert, Tamara and her guests began to chat about the ball and some of the attendees. They shared gossip about what people were wearing, tidbits of observed naughty behavior, and overall praise of the good time that was had by all. Finally, Sostor stood and told them that he had a reservation on the next Bubble Train and regretfully must take his leave. He asked his brother if he was also taking that train, but Sunan said no, he had a reservation on a later train. Seeming in a jovial mood, Sostor left the room to catch the train.

"Well," commented Sunan. "That could have been awkward, but it seemed to flow well. What do you think?"

"I agree," said Tamara. "Now we can exchange thoughts about our various defense projects. Sunan, why don't you begin?"

"I was able to contact my staff and preparations appear to be on schedule," he reported.

"But what are those preparations?" pressed Savea. "You haven't shared many details."

A page rushed into the room and gave Sunan an envelope. "This message just arrived for you, my Lord," he said.

Sunan quickly opened the envelope and read the contents. "Please excuse me, Your Majesty, Sisters," I must return to my kingdom. Apparently, I will be taking my brother's train after all," he explained as he rushed from the room.

"My goodness!" exclaimed Solange. "That was a sudden departure."

"Sudden and well-executed," added Tamara. "Let me share with you what I learned from touching the Brothers. When I handed Sostor his dessert dish, I pretended to stumble so that I could touch his hand. I was surprised at what I found out. At first, I sensed that he was pleased with his visit to our kingdom and proud that he had revealed nothing to me. Yet there was an undercurrent of alarm and panic. It was as if Sostor had two different souls!"

"How strange," commented Solange. "When we were

dancing, I had a somewhat similar feeling about him and didn't know what to make of it."

"Then when I led Sunan to a table after serving him," added Tamara, "I felt similar disjointed fragments from him which were nothing like the sensations that enveloped us when that tornado I caused raised us into the air, which were very positive and hopeful. Now he felt warm and loving externally, but there were waves of cold ruthlessness beneath the surface. I still don't understand the significance of that dichotomy."

"This is very disturbing, and now I have questions," Solange reflected. "I don't know what to believe. What was the spell that Sunan had you chant to remove his spell—and did it really do so? Additionally, was Sunan truly my lover and is his new role as your grandfather an accurate one or is it a magical ploy? I feel like the world has been turned upside down."

"If everything about the Brothers that we have supposedly learned and believed is of magical design, there is much more to discover," summarized Tamara. "What was it like when you and Savea were separated?"

Savea answered, "Before the separation, when we were one Super Being, we shared everything together. Afterward, I had a segment of our combined memories and abilities—and I assume that Solange received the rest. But it wasn't a negative experience. I still retained a shadow of what was given to her, so I still felt like a complete entity. Solange, what was it like for you?"

"It was the same," Solange answered. "I didn't feel incomplete, but I also no longer had some abilities that I later identified were under your control. Because we were now twins, I believe that certain traits and connections remain in place. This helps us work together and understand each other."

"Did you ever resent the separation or wonder if your other half received more benefits than you did?" asked Tamara.

"Yes," replied Savea. "No," responded Solange.

"Then I'm detecting a possible imbalance in the division you experienced," commented Tamara. "May I hold your hands for a moment?"

Each Sister held out a hand. When Tamara grasped the outstretched hands, she shivered and the crystal on her forehead glowed brightly. A rainbow beam shot down to the Sisters' hands and wrapped around them. The beam pulsated rapidly, then disappeared. Tamara asked," How are you feeling?"

"Complete," cried both Sisters at the same time.

"I feel just as I did when we were one Being," observed Savea.

"I feel the same," agreed Solange. "And now I understand the emotions you exhibited when you were so angry with me.

Thank you, Tamara. You have healed what we never realized needed healing!"

"I think we must re-examine what I discovered when I touched the Brothers in light of what you have just experienced. If the Brothers were similarly affected by an imbalance when they were changed from one Being into two, what does that say about what I found?" questioned Tamara. "And one more thing. Yesterday, you each had lunch with a Brother while I went to my bedroom to rest. Did you learn anything that you want to share?"

"Oh my," exclaimed Savea, "Did I ever! Sostor kept plying me with wine and sitting closer and closer to me. He kept bringing up in conversation how much we were alike and wouldn't working together be fun! I made sure to encourage his delusion and I pretended to be very interested in everything that he had to say!"

"Have you two set a wedding date yet?" joked Solange.

"Be serious, Sister," Savea shot back. "I'm trying to maintain a balance here, not lose my mind!"

"Noted," smiled Solange. "As for my luncheon experience, I had somehow expected Sunan to try to rekindle the wedding night relationship, but that certainly didn't happen. In fact, he seemed to be trying very hard to build a very proper interaction between us. There was no observable affection displayed at all. I was very puzzled."

"Hmm," Tamara. "Sometimes I wish I had some education in the psychological arts. All I can offer is a layperson's observations. Savea, your report makes me think that Sostor definitely wants to be your ally—or more to the point, wants you to be HIS ally. I don't believe emotion has anything to do with his behavior. That said, if my sense of a dual soul is to be believed and fear and panic is being suppressed by a desire to manipulate, what does that tell us?"

"You know, before the Brothers came to visit, I had a negative impression of Sostor and a positive one of Sunan," commented Solange. "What if those assessments were not accurate? What if goodness actually resides more in Sostor than in Sunan—but it is being dominated by a cold surface persona?"

Savea jumped in, "And the cold ruthlessness that Tamara felt below the surface in Sunan was being dominated by that warm and fuzzy exterior? I think we can assume that one of the Brothers visited you on your wedding night. The question is: Which one?"

"So are you saying that these various personality traits are mixed up in both Brothers? Do you recommend that we figure out how to restore the balance and see where the traits land? asked Tamara.

"Yes, that's exactly what I'm suggesting," replied Savea. "One more thing: Tamara, when you and Sunan were in that tornado together, what was your intuition telling you about him? Were you absolutely certain that what you were chanting was intended to break a spell? Could it possibly have been a magical cover-up that hid the truth from you, making you believe a lie? What if the dominated ruthlessness was able to break through then temporarily and Sunan was never really under a spell?"

"I think my head is beginning to hurt!" complained Tamara. "Wait a minute! There was a moment before dessert today when I was touching a hand of both Brothers. Can either of you put me in a trance so I can remember it more clearly?"

"No, but Dr. Angelus can. Let's send for him," Solange urged.

*   *   *   *   *

There was a soft knock at the door to the Private Dining Room and Dr. Angelus entered. "Your Majesty, Sisters, how can I be of service?"

Tamara quickly explained what she needed and Dr. Angelus escorted her to one of the couches so that she could recline. "Close your eyes, Your Majesty, and try to relax," Dr. Angelus intoned. "I'm going to say a chant now, the intent of which is to release the memory of that incident. When you awaken, you will remember everything and feel refreshed. All anxiety will be gone. Are you ready?"

"I am," Tamara sighed. She closed her eyes as he directed and listened as the sounds of chanting surrounded her. Dr. Angelus stretched out his hands and a golden haze covered Tamara. To his amazement, she began to levitate and drift across the room. Both Sisters gasped and told Dr. Angelus that she had done this before. As they watched, Tamara extended her arms and rainbows emerged from the crystals on her palms. Astonished, Dr. Angelus resumed his chanting and Tamara's body began rotating slowly. Tamara's bracelets began to glow and the golden haze was drawn into them. Tamara slowly drifted back to the couch and settled there. She sat up gingerly and smiled, "Thank you, Doctor. It seems that my crystals and bracelets contained a very clear memory of that occasion. Moreover, they were able to separate truth from falsehoods, so the resultant memory is clear and accurate."

"Your Majesty," said Dr. Angelus as he bowed deeply, "I have never seen anything like what I just witnessed. May I have your permission to withdraw and ponder it?"

"Of course," Tamara approved, "And thank you for your assistance."

Dr. Angelus left the room, shaking his head in absolute

bewilderment.

"What did you see?" cried Solange and Savea together.

Tamara smiled and clasped their hands. "I have much to share with you."

About the Author

After doing academic writing during my 20 years as Professor at the University of Wisconsin-Madison, I retired to Hawai'i in 1999. A decade later, I began being aware of an interesting fantasy story line in my mind and began writing it soon after. It was an occasional hobby for another decade and then the book became impatient with me and began to seriously nudge me. Since I began "listening" to the book, the writing has been a fun and all-encompassing part of my life.

Coming Soon

**Book 3
Masquerade**

**Book 4
Discoveries**

**Book 5
Gamesmanship**

**Book 6
Beginnings**

Scan the QR Code with Your Cell Phone to Order Books

www.ingramcontent.com/pod-product-compliance
Lightning Source LLC
Chambersburg PA
CBHW071309110426
42743CB00042B/1239